THE FOUNTAINWELL DRAMA SERIES

General Editors

T. A. DUNN

ANDREW GURR

JOHN HORDEN

A. NORMAN JEFFARES

R. L. C. LORIMER

Assistant General Editor

BRIAN W. M. SCOBIE

FRANCIS BEAUMONT

and

JOHN FLETCHER

THE MAID'S TRAGEDY

Edited by
ANDREW GURR

OLIVER & BOYD

EDINBURGH

1969

OLIVER AND BOYD LTD

Tweeddale Court
Edinburgh 1

822
BEA

First Published 1969

Hardback 05 001817 5
Paperback 05 001818 3

Printed in Great Britain by
Hazell Watson & Viney Ltd
Aylesbury, Bucks

ACKNOWLEDGEMENTS

I should like to thank Professor T. A. Dunn, who has acted with judgement and patience as Textual General Editor of this play, and Brian Scobie, whose technical persistence has been invaluable. And I should like to acknowledge a particular debt to Professor R. K. Turner, whose labours on the text of *The Maid's Tragedy* have provided a foundation for this edition which reaches in places nearly to its roof.

A. J. G.

Leeds
1968

CONTENTS

CRITICAL INTRODUCTION   1

A NOTE ON THE TEXT   9

THE MAID'S TRAGEDY   14

TEXTUAL NOTES   101

COMMENTARY   113

BIBLIOGRAPHY   118

GLOSSARY   121

CRITICAL INTRODUCTION

The Maid's Tragedy appeared at the height of the collaboration between Beaumont and Fletcher. It is first heard of obliquely on 31 Oct. 1611, when the Master of the Revels signified his approval of another play manuscript by writing on it "This second Maydens tragedy (for it hath no name inscribed) may wth the reformations bee acted publikely."[1] It would appear from this that *The Maid's Tragedy* had recently passed through his hands, as a preliminary to public performance. When it was written in relation to the other plays of the collaboration is not known, but it most likely followed *Philaster*, and probably *A King and No King*, which was also passed for acting in 1611, and was performed at Court that Christmas. The first direct record of *The Maid's Tragedy* appears on 20 May 1613 when John Hemynges on behalf of the King's Company was paid for thirteen plays, including *The Maid's Tragedy*, *Philaster*, *A King and No King*, and five plays of Shakespeare, presented by his company as part of the celebrations for the wedding of the Princess Elizabeth to the Elector Palatine.[2]

The partnership of Beaumont and Fletcher has prompted a variety of tests to ascertain which author wrote what parts of the play. The latest and most stringent is that of Cyrus Hoy,[3] mainly using spelling characteristics. Even his tests, as Clifford Leech[4] has pointed out, are less effective in distinguishing Fletcher from Beaumont than from Massinger and the later collaborators. *The Faithful Shepherdess*, a play certainly entirely Fletcher's, would on Hoy's tests be more or less all Beaumont's. Moreover, in the case of *The Maid's Tragedy*, and probably those of other plays in which Fletcher collaborated with Beaumont, the final version of the play seems to have been copied out in its entirety by Beaumont, who of course used his own spellings. Hoy's conclusions however, based here on verbal parallels, concur

[1] See E. K. Chambers, *The Elizabethan Stage* (4 vols, Oxford 1923), IV. 45.
[2] *Op. cit.* IV. 180.
[3] Cyrus Hoy, "The Shares of Fletcher and his Collaborators in the Beaumont and Fletcher Canon (III)", in *Studies in Bibliography*, XI (1958), p. 94.
[4] Clifford Leech, *The John Fletcher Plays*, p. 25.

with those of his predecessors on the whole in ascribing not only the final text but the bulk of the composition to Beaumont, with Fletcher contributing only II. II, IV. I, and V. I and II. These scenes, though comprising little over one fifth of the whole, include both the climactic scene of Melantius converting Evadne from sin to repentance, and its eventual *dénouement*, the King's murder.

If Hoy's ascription is accurate, various pieces of evidence throw light on the pattern of collaboration and the relationship between the authors. For instance, there are the revisions which suggest that Beaumont was controller of the final copy;[5] and in broader terms an analysis of the issues set out in the play suggests that they were Beaumont's rather than Fletcher's. Seen as a play questioning the implications of absolute monarchy, which in important respects it clearly is, it stands at odds with Fletcher's own *Valentinian* of 1612–14, which Mincoff sees as "an attack on his partner's principles, or a piece of atonement for his own share in *The Maid's Tragedy*."[6] On the other hand, in *Philaster*, where Hoy finds the authors with a more evenly balanced partnership than in *The Maid's Tragedy*, the questioning of absolutism is even more heavily marked. Fletcher can presumably be allowed to have shifted his political views even in these few years.

Such questions aside, the collaboration was so close and efficient that no loose ends, incongruities between one scene and another, or differences in the basic concept can be distinguished anywhere in the play. The very difficulty of ascribing the different parts of the play to each author is a tribute to their joint craftsmanship.

The Maid's Tragedy has that anomaly amongst Elizabethan trage-dies, an original plot. Both the success of the collaboration in its craftsmanship and in its literary accomplishment depend upon this fact. Much of the collaborators' ingenuity was spent on laying down a strong story-line within which exist complexities, not of imagery and character but of situations, where a question could be posed and resolved in dramatic terms. This is the primary reason why the plays of the collaboration owe so little directly to literary sources. *The Maid's Tragedy* does take its place within one major tradition of

---

[5] See for instance Textual Note to II. II. 13.

[6] Marco Mincoff, "Fletcher's Early Tragedies", in *Renaissance Drama*, VII (1964), p. 75.

Elizabethan and Jacobean drama, in its adaptation for the stage of some of the main features of the prose romances, and of Sidney's *Arcadia* (1590) in particular. The *Arcadia* gave Fletcher the actual plot of his *Cupid's Revenge*, written in or about 1608; the debts of *The Maid's Tragedy* are less immediate, drawing on *Arcadia* and its peer, D'Urfée's *L'Astree* (1610), not for the plot, which owes its conception to something independent of a literary source, but for the use of situational complications as a determining factor in the story.[7] The use of stock characters in improbably complicated situations, the least of which might involve, say, a courtier wooing on behalf of a friend becoming himself the object of the lady's passion (like *Twelfth Night* without the comedy), is basic to *Arcadia* and *L'Astrée*, whether simply in order to exploit the emotional extremes which arise from such situations, or to utilise them for pointing moral or psychological insights. This was the kind of narrative form and convention which, combined with obvious debts for dramatic devices to Shakespeare, Beaumont and Fletcher took over for the chief plays of the collaboration.

Even here though the debt can be overstated. Sidney and D'Urfée created the literary fashion which the collaborators took as their dramatic medium; but they provided the vehicle rather than the tenor of the metaphor which the play constitutes. Its real origin can be seen in the implications of Fuller's anecdote about Fletcher mulling over the first ideas for a tragedy, and proposing *"to Kill the King therein"*[8]

It has often been said that the play's title is misleading. Aspatia, the only maid to whom it could apply, is a victim of the events in the tragedy; but it is no more her tragedy alone than *Hamlet* is Ophelia's. If any title could summarise the major concerns of the play it is one of Thomas Rymer's alternatives, *The Lustful King*. The whole action of the play stems from the initial circumstance of the King's having made Evadne his mistress. From that comes the situation with which the play opens, where the King has taken the young Amintor from his betrothed Aspatia, and led him to marry Evadne, in order to cover

[7] Marco Mincoff, "The Social Background of Beaumont and Fletcher", in *English Miscellany*, 1 (1950), p. 24.
[8] Thomas Fuller, *The Worthies of England* (1662), Oooi[v]. Fuller does not name the play to which the anecdote refers.

their adultery. Melantius, as Evadne's brother and Amintor's bosom friend, is recalled from the wars to the wedding. When after the wedding Amintor has learnt of his new wife's dishonour and the King's deceit, and in his misery has revealed the situation to Melantius, the two men find themselves in almost precisely the same position, as husband and brother of Evadne, with regard to the man who has dishonoured her. Both their honours are tainted by his shaming of Evadne. But their position is complicated, made an inextricable dilemma, by the fact of the adulterer's being the King, to whom their allegiance as honourable men is due. Their different reactions to the dilemma, Amintor to suffer in shameful silence, Melantius to take revenge, and the consequences of these reactions, compose the rest of the play. In the process the ethics of the conflict between personal honour and public duty are examined, and the hidden point of Fuller's anecdote made clear. The killing of the King is the peg on which the examination hangs.

The given title of the play is not entirely inappropriate, however. The play is certainly not centrally the tragedy of Aspatia, but it is not purely and centrally anyone else's either. It is not a tragedy in the usual sense; it has no single great figure brought low by Fortune's wheel or Aristotle's peripeteia. The starting-point of the play is a moral problem, private and political, presented in terms rather of a situation than of an individual. It involves a construction of attitudes to the King's crime and a pair of alternative resolutions for the problem thus presented. For this purpose only attitudes are needed, not characters. The King himself is never more than a lustful (and with it a jealous) monarch. Amintor is an honest youth, Melantius a soldier turned revenger, Evadne a lustful (and ambitious) woman, Aspatia a wronged maid. Characterisation need bear no more weight than this. The various attitudes are presented unambiguously: Amintor may be maddened by his rage against the King but never questions the honest man's duty of loyalty; his youth is stressed in revision[9]. Evadne needs only a few lines of frank speaking to the King to sketch in her motivation[10]. Melantius is the man of action who will not, as Amintor does, wait for the Gods to "speake to" the King, but takes his revenge and suffers for it. The play's extraordinary theatrical qualities, the complexities of the dialogue and the *coups de théâtre*

[9] *The Maid's Tragedy*, hereafter cited as *M.T.*, II. II. 102.
[10] *M.T.*, III. I. 198-9.

come from the situation, not from any complexities of characterisation or dramatic irony. Such famous lines as Evadne's "A maidenhead *Amintor* at my yeares?"[11], and Melantius' "They must weepe *Diphilus*"[12] gain their cogency from the element of surprise, of the contrast between the situation as it exists on stage before the line is spoken, and after. The tragedy similarly exists in the situation, the ethical dilemma, not in the characters.

Intellectually the core of the play is made up of familiar elements, the two absolutes of monarchic right and personal honour. The political aspect is more or less that of *Richard II*, a rightful but unjust monarch confronting his subjects with the choice of suffering in dishonour or taking action against him and undergoing the retributions of the usurper or revenger. "Honour" is the key concept in the play, applied in one form or other more than forty times. It, too, is familiar enough in plays of this period, but its applications here are as complex as the situation by which it is illuminated, and bear close analysis. It had two main head-meanings in the seventeenth century, reputation, and honourableness or virtue.[13] The former was the more common early in the century, particularly the reputation of high rank. The second meaning was rare at the outset, but usage was fluid, and it increased to become the dominant sense in the Restoration. Beaumont and Fletcher markedly anticipate later attitudes in stressing the personal honour of family prestige or duelling rather than the public reputation of high rank. Both are present in *The Maid's Tragedy*, though the dilemma is put in terms of the personal aspect. Basically the word is used as the "dishonour" caused to husband, brother, and self by the loss of Evadne's virtue, (although to Amintor at times this seems to be as much public opinion as self-esteem). The pattern of usage however involves not only "honour" and its derivatives but also in some contexts the term "honesty" with its related forms. "Honest" seems in places to be serving as the adjective for the "personal virtue" aspect of "honour". Honour as personal reputation is used of Amintor, once actually with "reputation" as a synonym, and as family reputation of and by Melantius. Sexual virtue as "honour" appears with reference to Evadne (Amintor's sexual virtue before his marriage is called "honesty").

---

[11] *M.T.*, II. I. 220.   [12] *M.T.*, III. II. 299.
[13] C. L. Barber, *The Idea of Honour in the English Drama* 1591–1700 (*Gothen-burg Studies in English* VI, Göteborg 1957), pp. 330 sqq.

Honour in its aspect of "honesty" shows most neatly the nature of the dilemma Amintor and Melantius find themselves in. "Honest" Amintor, though forced into dissembling over his marriage to Evadne, is unable because of his honesty to take up arms against his king. When he is so driven by his torment over the King's treatment that he is on the point of rushing in pursuit of him with drawn sword, Melantius, in order to preserve his own more subtle plot, reiterates the King's name to check him, adding in an aside "I know hees honest, / And this will worke with him."[14] Melantius, on the other hand, immediately he has discovered his dishonour undertakes to trick Calianax out of his possession of the Fort by a most ingenious piece of dishonesty. The change in his character from "honest" blunt soldier to cunning deceiver, not only tricking Calianax but giving the lie direct to Amintor his friend, serves to underline the nature of the course he has chosen. Morality as well as the revenge convention ensures that he will never live happily having undertaken such a course. In the conflict of absolutes, each chooses one and suffers by the other. Amintor says, at the end of the scene where the dilemma is shown at its nicest,

> The thing that we call honour beares us all
> Headlong into sinne, and yet it selfe is nothing.[15]

It bears Melantius into sin, as he makes himself "mine owne justice to revenge", and like all revengers, he ends in suffering:

> on lustfull Kings
> Unlookt for suddaine deaths from God are sent,
> But curst is he that is their instrument.[16]

As noted above, *The Maid's Tragedy* was performed by the King's Men at Court within a year or two of its composition, a reliable sign

---

[14] *M.T.*, IV. II. 350–1.

[15] *M.T.*, IV. II. 358–9.

[16] *M.T.*, V. III. 316–8. A study of the social and political background to Beaumont and Fletcher can be found in the sixth chapter of J. F. Danby's *Poets on Fortune's Hill*, a book which also contains an excellent analysis of what Danby calls the "moral puns" of situation in the play. Clifford Leech (*The John Fletcher Plays*) relates the play and its main issues in detail to the other works of the two collaborators.

of its contemporary esteem.[17] It was possibly performed there again in 1619 or 1620, and was certainly there in 1630–1631 and in 1636. It was evidently kept in the King's Company repertoire for most of the Company's last thirty years. In the Interregnum the Calianax scenes were made into a droll or farce called *The Testy Lord*, for the Red Bull. It was revived in 1660 and 1661, when Pepys saw it, as he did four times more before 1668. It was probably banned by Charles for portraying the murder of a monarch on stage, and was only performed again when adapted by Waller, who made three attempts to change the fifth act into something acceptably monarchist. Betterton played Melantius in 1706 and 1710 at the Haymarket, and it was produced on fourteen more occasions in the first half of the eighteenth century, after which it disappeared. An adaptation by Macready was acted at the Haymarket in 1837. In the twentieth century it has not been given a major production.

[17] There is little doubt that Beaumont and Fletcher wrote their plays for performance by the King's Men both at the Globe, their 'public' or open theatre, and at the Blackfriars, their small indoor 'private' theatre. The use of the Blackfriars was granted to the company in 1608, and its existence seems in various ways to have shaped the kind of play produced for it by Shakespeare as well as Beaumont and Fletcher. It was probably not so much the different kind of theatre as the more exclusively aristocratic audience which influenced their plays, notably in the utilization of such devices as the inset masque. G. E. Bentley ("Shakespeare and the Blackfriars Theatre", in *Shakespeare Survey*, 1 (1948), pp. 38–50) and Marco Mincoff ("The Social Background of Beaumont and Fletcher" in, *op. cit.*) examine the question in detail; the truth probably lies somewhere between them.

A NOTE ON THE TEXT

The copy for *The Maid's Tragedy* was entered in the Stationers' Register on 28 Apr. 1619, to the booksellers Richard Higgenbotham and Francis Constable,[1] and the first quarto, with variant imprints for the two on the title page, was printed in the same year by Nicholas Okes. A second quarto, "newly perused, augmented, and inlarged", was printed for Constable alone by George Purslowe in 1622. Four more quartos appeared, in 1630, 1638, 1641 and 1660, before the play joined the second folio in 1679. The second quarto was printed from Q1, with the addition of about eighty lines and numerous minor verbal and punctuation changes, largely authorial. Q3 was printed from Q2 with a few changes which some editors have taken to be authorial. Subsequent quartos and the folio are reprints of earlier editions.

The copy-text for this edition of the play is Q1, from which all other editions were printed, with additions and emendations taken from Q2[2]. Q3's alterations are slight, and almost certainly made not by the authors but by Richard Hawkins, who was assigned the copyright by both the original publishers in 1629, and who added a prefatory poem to his 1630 edition. The chief problems are, first, the nature of the manuscript used to set Q1, and, secondly, the nature of the second manuscript, used to annotate a copy of Q1 for the Q2 edition. R. K. Turner jr[3] has conjectured that Q1 was set from foul papers untouched by the theatre, on the evidence of misreadings and other indications that the compositor was handling a difficult manuscript containing illegibilities and cancellations. The passages which appear in Q2 but not in Q1 are not in the main either theatrical cuts made in the Q1 copy, nor accidental cancellations in Q1, but passages added in revision to the manuscript used for Q2, and added to an already

[1] *A Transcript of the Registers of the Company of Stationers Of London*, 1554–1640 *A.D.*, ed. E. Arber (5 vols, London 1875–94).

[2] Robert K. Turner, jr, "The Relationship of *The Maid's Tragedy* Q1 and Q2", in *P.B.S.A.*, LI (1957), pp. 322–7.

[3] Robert K. Turner jr, "A Textual Study of Beaumont and Fletcher's *The Maid's Tragedy*" (2 vols), pp. 419 sqq. Unpublished dissertation (University of Virginia) 1958.

completed text. The compositorial difficulties of the Q1 copy are made apparent by the corrections in Q2, which Turner considers was published with the aid of the fair copy, a final manuscript version transcribed in full by one of the authors, probably Beaumont, since the linguistic features are uniform throughout, and containing revisions not only stylistic but also of stage business and the ascription of minor speeches. However, to say that, compositorial errors aside, the differences between Q1 and Q2 are those between foul papers and fair copy is to oversimplify on the basis of a misused and too neatly categorising pair of terms. It is fairly clear that the copy used for the Q2 annotations was a later version of the play than the Q1 copy, but their difference is more that between two states of fair copy than that between foul papers and fair copy. There is only one suggestion of the false start usually thought characteristic of foul papers[4], and that survives through both quartos. All the major additions[5] in Q2 are intrusive on the sense of Q1. Both manuscripts seem to be in the same hand, since none of Fletcher's spellings appear even in the Q1 version of the scenes thought to be by him. The most that can be said is that the Q2 variants represent revisions of the Q1 text, and that therefore the Q2 annotator must have used a manuscript in some way posterior to that used as copy for Q1. Neither manuscript has any of the characteristics of a scribal transcript, so we must conclude that for some reason Beaumont himself transcribed the play twice. Since one copy would probably have gone to the players, and from them to form the basis of either Q1 or Q2,[6] Beaumont may have decided to keep a copy for himself, in a version which eventually also reached the printer. A pair of manuscripts in a similar relation to one another lie behind the two authoritative quartos of *Philaster*. Beaumont was dead three years before the first *Maid's Tragedy* quarto appeared, so he could not have been himself the annotator. There has never been any question of the Q2 revisions not being authorial, and little that they are Beaumont's. All previous editors have in fact adopted Q2 as

---

[4] *M.T.*, v. iii. 182.

[5] *M.T.*, i. i. 101–4; i. ii. 148–57 and 256–71; ii. i. 79–98; ii. ii. 18–30; and iii. i. 228–33.

[6] Copy held by the players need not have been marked for the theatre. See Fredson Bowers, *On Editing Shakespeare and the Elizabethan Dramatists*, pp. 11 sqq. A number of King's Company plays made their way to the printer between 1619 and 1622, presumably from the theatre.

their copy-text, since this clearly represents the final state of the text as passed by at least one of the collaborators.

The nature of the authorial afterthoughts can be illustrated neatly enough by one variant where Beaumont in the final copy seemingly felt obliged to modify Fletcher's text. In II. II. 13, Fletcher made Aspatia say of one of her women that she had "a metled temper, fit for stamp", a neat image, but one not consonant with her complaisant character as Beaumont saw it, for in the final copy "metled" is altered to "easie", losing part of the conceit for the sake of the dramatic context.

If this hypothesis of the manuscript source for each quarto is accepted, assessment of likely compositorial error in the transmission of the text becomes relatively straightforward. Q1 was set in two parts, with a clear break between sheets G and H, and different pairs of skeleton formes;[7] possibly sheets H–L were printed in a shop other than Okes's.[8] Although it was evidently a difficult text to set, there are press variants in only four formes, and many obvious errors were passed over even in the formes which were corrected.[9] All the Q1 corrections were obvious and have been adopted for this edition. Q2 was set from a copy of Q1 containing the corrected states of all four formes. It was set by three compositors, whose practices in handling copy and likelihood of error are known.[10] Three formes contain a total of four press variants in Q2, all but one concerning punctuation. All press variants have been recorded in the textual notes.

The important characteristics of *The Maid's Tragedy's* text therefore are, essentially, that both the copy-text and the emendations in Q2 are based on fair copy, the emendations being either corrected misreadings or last-minute tinkering rather than proper revision. Except for the punctuation, which is markedly light and erratic in Q1 and was thoroughly and accurately overhauled in Q2, there are no

[7] Robert K. Turner jr, "The Printing of Beaumont and Fletcher's *The Maid's Tragedy* Q1 (1619)", in *S.B.*, XIII (1960), pp. 199–200.

[8] See H. B. Norland, "The Text of *The Maid's Tragedy*", *P.B.S.A.*, LXI (1967), p. 177.

[9] *Ibid.* p. 218. The list of press variants given by Turner is accurate for the two copies in Britain except that the outer forme of sheet E in the Dyce copy is in the uncorrected state, not the corrected.

[10] Turner, "A Textual Study of Beaumont and Fletcher's *The Maid's Tragedy*", in *op. cit.*, pp. 482 sqq.

consistent differences between the two texts. No theatre influence is shown in either text, though some of the revisions (the change from "your dores" to "the dore" in IV. I. II, for instance) might have been made with one eye on the staging. And three of the songs, one in the masque and two in the scene of Evadne's disrobing, seem to be late insertions, conceivably at the request of the players.

Certain characteristics of the copy-text have been retained in this edition although doubtfully authorial; for instance the change in the spelling of Calianax's name in the latter part of the play, after the break in the setting of Q1 (IV. II onwards). On the other hand, several Q2 additions which should be verse and which appear to have been inserted by the annotator as prose and set in prose by the compositor have been reversified. In the textual notes, where of two indifferent variants the Q2 text has been preferred to Q1 without any reason being given, it may be assumed that it is considered to be an authorial revision. In other cases correction of compositorial errors of anticipation and recollection, eyeskip, misreading, or memorial error in either text is readily recognisable as such. The punctuation except where noted has been taken throughout from Q2, since it received careful attention in the fair copy which provided the Q2 alterations; although one must acknowledge a doubt whether the revision in Q2 is necessarily Beaumont's. The following silent alterations have been made for this edition: (a) the letter "s" has been substituted for "long s" wherever it occurs; (b) the complementary letters "i" and "j", and "u" and "v" have been interchanged in conformity with modern practice; (c) all abbreviations, including ampersands, have been expanded; (d) faulty capitalisation (at the beginning of a line of verse, or at the beginning of a proper name) has been regularised in accordance with normal usage; (e) speech-prefixes are set in caps and small caps, and are given in full and always in the same form; numerals in speech prefixes are spelt in full; (f) the characters' names have been similarly normalised in stage directions; and (g) additional stage directions, or additions to existing ones, have been provided within pointed brackets; in some places, square brackets have been used to distinguish original stage directions from the text proper where there is possibility of confusion.

All other departures from the copy-text are recorded in the Textual Notes, which are to be found in two places; those which significantly affect the meaning of a passage at the foot of the relevant page, and all others in the section at the back of the book. These notes do not reproduce the readings of the 1630 quarto or subsequent texts, unless they have been adopted into the present text.

DRAMATIS PERSONAE

KING

LISIPPUS, *brother to the* KING

AMINTOR

EVADNE, *wife to* AMINTOR

MELANTIUS ⎫
          ⎬ *brothers to* EVADNE
DIPHILUS ⎭

ASPATIA, *troth-plight wife to* AMINTOR

CALIANAX, *an old humorous Lord, and father to* ASPATIA

CLEON ⎫
       ⎬ *gentlemen*
STRATO ⎭

DIAGORAS, *a servant*

ANTIPHILA ⎫
          ⎬ *waiting gentlewomen to* ASPATIA
OLIMPIAS ⎭

DULA, *a Lady*

NIGHT   ⎫
         ⎪
CYNTHIA ⎪
         ⎬ *maskers*
NEPTUNE ⎪
         ⎪
EOLUS   ⎭

LORDS, GENTLEMEN, LADIES, SERVANTS, MESSENGER

ACT I

SCENE I

Enter CLEON, STRATO, LISIPPUS, DIPHILUS.

CLEON.   The rest are making ready sir.

STRATO.   So let them, theres time enough.

DIPHILUS.   You are the brother to the King my Lord, wee'le take your word.

LISIPPUS.   *Strato* thou hast some skill in poetrie, what think'st   5
thou of a maske, will it be well?

STRATO.   As well as masks can be.

LISIPPUS.   As masks can be?

STRATO.   Yes, they must commend their King, and speake in
praise of the assembly, blesse the Bride and groome, in person   10
of some God, they'r tied to rules of flatterie.

CLEON.   See good my Lord who is return'd.

Enter MELANTIUS.

LISIPPUS.   Noble *Melantius*, the land by me
    Welcomes thy vertues home to *Rhodes*,
    Thou that with blood abroad buyest us our peace.   15
    The breath of Kings is like the breath of gods:
    My brother wisht thee here, and thou art here:
    He will be too kinde, and wearie thee
    With often welcomes: but the time doth give thee
    A welcome, above his, or all the worlds.   20

MELANTIUS.   My Lord, my thankes, but these scratcht limbes
    of mine,
    Have spoke my love and truth unto my friends,
    More then my tongue ere could, my mind's the same

I. I. 2 STRATO]. LYS. Q1; *Stra.* Q2. *Daniel etc. accept* Q1, *on the assumption that
Lisippus replies when addressed by Cleon. But Strato's character is sketched through-
out as that of a forthright cynic, and it would be in character for him to interrupt the
King's brother.*

14 home to *Rhodes*,] Q2; home, Q1. *This reference, which creates metrical difficulties, was probably added in revision to clarify the locale of the story.*

It ever was to you; where I finde worth,
I love the keeper, till he let it goe,   25
And then I follow it.
DIPHILUS.   Haile worthy brother,
  He that rejoyces not at your returne
  In safetie, is mine enemy for ever.
MELANTIUS.   I thanke thee *Diphilus*: but thou art faultie,   30
  I sent for thee to exercise thine armes
  With me at *Patria*: thou camst not *Diphilus*;
  Twas ill.
DIPHILUS.   My noble brother, my excuse
  Is my Kings strict command, which you my Lord   35
  Can witnesse with me.
LISIPPUS.   Tis most true *Melantius*,
  He might not come till the solemnities
  Of this great match were past.
DIPHILUS.   Have you heard of it?   40
MELANTIUS.   Yes, I have given cause to those, that here
  Envy my deedes abroad, to call me gamesome,
  I have no other busines here at *Rhodes*.
LISIPPUS.   We have a maske to night,
  And you must tread a souldiers measure.   45
MELANTIUS.   These soft and silken warres are not for me,
  The musicke must be shrill and all confus'd,
  That stirs my blood, and then I dance with Armes:
  But is *Amintor* wed?
DIPHILUS.   This day.   50
MELANTIUS.   All joyes upon him, for he is my friend:
  Wonder not that I call a man so young my friend;
  His worth is great, valiant he is and temperate,
  And one that never thinkes his life his owne,
  If his friend neede it: when he was a boy,   55
  As oft as I return'd (as without boast
  I brought home conquest) he would gaze upon me,
  And view me round, to finde in what one limbe
  The vertue lay to doe those things he heard,
  Then would he wish to see my sword, and feele   60
  The quicknesse of the edge, and in his hand

35 strict] Q2; straight Q1.

Weigh it, he oft would make me smile at this;
His youth did promise much, and his ripe yeares
Will see it all perform'd.

Enter ASPATIA *passing by.*

Haile Maide and Wife.   65
Thou faire *Aspatia*, may the holy knot
That thou hast tied to day, last till the hand
Of age undoe't, mayst thou bring a race
Unto *Amintor*, that may fill the world
Successively with souldiers.   70
ASPATIA.   My hard fortunes
Deserve not scorne, for I was never proud
When they were good.

                              Exit ASPATIA.

MELANTIUS.   Howes this?
LISIPPUS.   You are mistaken, for she is not married.   75
MELANTIUS.   You said *Amintor* was.
DIPHILUS.   Tis true, but
MELANTIUS.   Pardon me, I did receive
Letters at *Patria* from my *Amintor*
That he should marie her.   80
DIPHILUS.   And so it stood,
In all opinion long, but your arrivall
Made me imagine you had heard the change.
MELANTIUS.   Who has he taken then?
LISIPPUS.   A Ladie sir,   85
That beares the light above her, and strikes dead
With flashes of her eye, the faire *Evadne*
Your vertuous sister.
MELANTIUS.   Peace of heart betwixt them,
But this is strange.   90
LISIPPUS.   The King my brother did it
To honour you, and these solemnities
Are at his charge.
MELANTIUS.   Tis royall like himselfe,

But I am sad, my speech beares so infortunate a sound   95
To beautifull *Aspatia*: there is rage
Hid in her fathers breast, Calianax
Bent long against me, and 'a should not thinke,
If I could call it backe, that I would take
So base revenges as to scorne the state   100
Of his neglected daughter:
Holds he still his greatnesse with the king?
LISIPPUS.   Yes, but this Lady walkes
Discontented, with her watrie eyes bent on the earth:
The unfrequented woods are her delight,   105
And when she sees a bancke stucke full of flowers,
Shee with a sigh will tell
Her servants, what a prittie place it were
To burie lovers in, and make her maides
Pluck 'em, and strow her over like a corse.   110
She carries with her an infectious griefe,
That strikes all her beholders, she will sing
The mournfulst things that ever eare hath heard,
And sigh, and sing againe, and when the rest
Of our young Ladyes in their wanton blood,   115
Tell mirthfull tales in course that fill the roome
With laughter, she will with so sad a looke
Bring forth a storie of the silent death
Of some forsaken virgin, which her griefe
Will put in such a phrase, that ere she end   120
Shee'le send them weeping one by one away.
MELANTIUS.   She has a brother under my command
Like her, a face as womanish as hers,
But with a spirit that hath much outgrowne
The number of his yeares.   125

Enter AMINTOR.

CLEON.   My Lord the Bridegroome.
MELANTIUS.   I might run fiercely, not more hastily
Upon my foe: I love thee well *Amintor*,
My mouth is much too narrow for my heart,
I joy to looke upon those eyes of thine,   130

Thou art my friend, but my disordred speech
Cuts off my love.

AMINTOR.   Thou art *Melantius*.
　　All love is spoke in that, a sacrifice
　　To thanke the gods, *Melantius* is return'd   135
　　In safty, victory sits on his sword
　　As she was wont; may she build there, and dwell,
　　And may thy armour be as it hath beene,
　　Onely thy valour and thine innocence.
　　What endlesse treasures would our enemies give,   140
　　That I might hold thee still thus!

MELANTIUS.   I am poore in words, but credit me, young man
　　Thy mother could no more but weep, for joy to see thee
　　After long absence: all the wounds I have,
　　Fetcht not so much away, nor all the cries   145
　　Of widdowed mothers: but this is peace,
　　And that was warre.

AMINTOR.   Pardon thou holy god
　　Of marriage bed, and frowne not, I am for'st
　　In answere of such noble teares as those,   150
　　To weepe upon my wedding day.

MELANTIUS.   I feare thou art growne too fickle, for I heare
　　A Lady mournes for thee, men say to death,
　　Forsaken of thee, on what tearmes I know not.

AMINTOR.   She had my promise, but the King forbad it,   155
　　And made me make this worthy change, thy sister,
　　Accompanied with graces about her,
　　With whom I long to loose my lusty youth,
　　And grow olde in her armes.

MELANTIUS.   Be prosperous.   160

Enter MESSENGER.

MESSENGER.   My Lord the maskers rage for you.
LISIPPUS.   We are gone, *Cleon, Straio, Diphilus.*
AMINTOR.   Weele all attend you.

　　　　　　　　Exeunt LISIPPUS, CLEON, STRATO, DIPHILUS
　　　　　　　　　　　　〈*and* MESSENGER〉.

We shall trouble you with our solemnities.

MELANTIUS.   Not so *Amintor.*   165
   But if you laugh at my rude carriage
   In peace, il'e doe as much for you in warre
   When you come thither: but I have a mistresse
   To bring to your delights, rough though I am,
   I have a mistresse and she has a heart   170
   She saies, but trust me, it is stone, no better,
   There is no place that I can challenge:
   But you stand still, and here my way lies.

                                Exeunt.

⟨ACT I⟩

⟨SCENE II⟩

Enter CALIANAX, *with* DIAGORAS.

CALIANAX.   *Diagoras* looke to the dores better for shame: you
  let in all the world, and anon the King will raile at me: why very
  well said, by *Jove* the King will have the show i'th Court.
DIAGORAS.   Why doe you sweare so my Lord? You know heele
  have it here.   5
CALIANAX.   By this light if he be wise, he will not.
DIAGORAS.   And if he will not be wise, you are forsworne.
CALIANAX.   One may sweat his heart out with swearing, and get
  thankes on no side, ile be gone, look too't who will.
DIAGORAS.   My Lord, I shall never keepe them out. Pray stay,   10
  your lookes will terrifie them.
CALIANAX.   My lookes terrifie them, you coxcomely asse you, ile
  be judgd by all the company, whether thou hast not a worse face
  then I.
DIAGORAS.   I meane because they know you, and your office.   15
CALIANAX.   Office, I would I could put it off, I am sure I sweat
  quite through my office, I might have made room at my daughters

   172 challenge,] Q2; challenge gentlemen, Q1. Q1, *which has Melantius address the
Courtiers, is the text which gives them an exit ten lines before;* Q2 *which omits the exit
also omits the address: probably an authorial muddle.*

   I. II. 8 may sweat ... out] may sweare his heart out Q2; must sweat out his
heart Q1. *The* Q1 *compositor misread* may, *and created a transposition error; and* Q2
anticipated or misread sweat.

wedding, they ha neere kild her amongst them. And now I must
doe service for him that hath forsaken her, serve that will.

Exit CALIANAX.

DIAGORAS.   Hee's so humerous since his daughter was for-   20
saken: hark, hark, there, there, so, so, codes, codes.

Knock within.

What now?
MELANTIUS.   [*within*] Open the dore.
DIAGORAS.   Who's there?
MELANTIUS.   ⟨*within*⟩ *Melantius.*   25
DIAGORAS.   I hope your Lord-ship brings no troope with you,
for if you doe, I must returne them.

Enter MELANTIUS *and a* LADY.

MELANTIUS.   None but this Lady sir.
DIAGORAS.   The Ladies are all plac'd above, save those that
come in the Kings troope, the best of *Rhodes* sit there, and theres   30
roome.
MELANTIUS.   I thanke you sir: when I have seene you placed
madam, I must attend the King, but the maske done, ile waite on
you againe.

Exit MELANTIUS ⟨*and*⟩ LADY *other dore.*

DIAGORAS.   Stand backe there, roome for my Lord *Melantius*,   35
pray beare back, this is no place for such youthes and their truls,
let the dores shut agen: I, do your heads itch? ile scratch them
for you: so now thrust and hang: againe, who i'st now, I cannot
blame my Lord *Calianax* for going away, would he were here, he
would run raging amongst them, and breake a dozen wiser heads   40
than his own in the twinckling of an eye: what's the newes now?
⟨VOICE⟩ [*within*] I pray you can you helpe mee to the speech of the
maister Cooke?
DIAGORAS.   If I open the dore ile cooke some of your calves
heads. Peace rogues. —againe, —who i'st?   45
MELANTIUS.   [*within*] *Melantius.*

Enter CALIANAX.

CALIANAX.   Let him not in.
DIAGORAS.   O my Lord a must,

Enter MELANTIUS.

make roome there for my Lord, is your Lady plast?
MELANTIUS.   Yes sir, I thanke you: my Lord *Calianax*, well met?   50
Your causelesse hate to me I hope is buried.
CALIANAX.   Yes I doe service for your sister here,
That brings mine owne poore child to timelesse death,
She loves your friend *Amintor*, such another false hearted
Lord as you.   55
MELANTIUS.   You doe me wrong,
A most unmanly one, and I am slow
In taking vengeance, but be well advis'd.
CALIANAX.   It may be so: who plac'd the Lady there so neere the
presence of the King?   60
MELANTIUS.   I did.
CALIANAX.   My Lord she must not sit there.
MELANTIUS.   Why?
CALIANAX.   The place is kept for women of more worth.
MELANTIUS.   More worth then she, it misbecomes your age,   65
And place to be thus womanish, forbeare,
What you have spoke I am content to thinke
The palsey shooke your tongue to.
CALIANAX.   Why tis well if I stand here to place mens wenches.
MELANTIUS.   I shall forget this place, thy age, my safety, and   70
through all, cut that poore sickly weeke thou hast to live away
from thee.
CALIANAX.   Nay I know you can fight for your whore.
MELANTIUS.   Bate me the King, and be hee flesh and blood
A lies that sayes it, thy mother at fifteene   75
Was black and sinfull to her.
DIAGORAS.   Good my Lord.
MELANTIUS.   Some god pluck threescore yeares from that fond
man,
That I may kill him, and not staine mine honor,
It is the curse of souldiers, that in peace   80
They shall be braved by such ignoble men,
As (if the land were troubled) would with teares

And knees beg succor from 'em, would that blood
(That sea of blood) that I have lost in fight,
Were running in thy veines, that it might make thee　　85
Apt to say lesse, or able to maintaine,
Shouldst thou say more, —This *Rhodes* I see is nought
But a place priviledg'd to doe men wrong.
CALIANAX.　I, you may say your pleasure.

Enter AMINTOR.

AMINTOR.　What vilde injurie　　　　　　　90
Has sturd my worthy friend, who is as slow
To fight with words as he is quicke of hand?
MELANTIUS.　That heape of age, which I should reverence
If it were temperate, but testie yeares
Are most contemptible.　　　　　　　　95
AMINTOR.　Good sir forbeare.
CALIANAX.　There is just such another as your selfe.
AMINTOR.　He will wrong you, or me, or any man,
And talke as if he had no life to loose
Since this our match: the King is comming in,　　100
I would not for more wealth than I enjoy
He should perceive you raging, he did heare
You were at difference now, which hastned him.
CALIANAX.　Make roome there.

　　　　　　　　　　　　Hoboyes play within.

Enter KING, EVADNE, ASPATIA, *Lords and Ladies.*

KING.　*Melantius* thou art welcome, and my love　　105
Is with thee still; but this is not a place
To brable in, *Calianax*, joyne hands.
CALIANAX.　He shall not have mine hand.
KING.　This is no time
To force you too't, I doe love you both,　　110
Calianax you looke well to your office,

105–6 my love/Is with thee] Q2; thy loue/Is with me Q1. *Two radically different meanings are offered here.* Q1 *seems unwarrantably to anticipate later developments in the story;* Q2 *accords with the King's subsequent gentle reproof.* Q1 *was probably a result of memorial error, but the possibility of an authorial revision akin to that in* I. I. 101–4 *cannot be ruled out.*

And you *Melantius* are welcome home,
Begin the maske.

MELANTIUS.   Sister I joy to see you, and your choyce,
You lookt with my eies when you tooke that man,   115
Be happy in him.

Recorders ⟨play within.⟩

EVADNE.   O my deerest brother,
Your presence is more joyfull then this day can be unto me.

Maske.
NIGHT *rises in mists.*

NIGHT.   Our raigne is come, for in the raging sea
The Sun is drownd, and with him fell the day: 120
Bright *Cinthia* heare my voyce, I am the night
For whom thou bearst about thy borrowed light,
Appeare, no longer thy pale visage shrowde,
But strike thy silver hornes quite through a cloud,
And send a beame upon my swarthie face,   125
By which I may discover all the place
And persons, and how many longing eies
Are come to waite on our solemnities.

Enter CYNTHIA.

How dull and black am I? I could not finde
This beautie without thee, I am so blinde,   130
Me thinkes they shew like to those easterne streaks,
That warne us hence before the morning breaks,
Back my pale servant, for these eies know how
To shoote farre more and quicker rayes then thou.

CYNTHIA.   Great Queen they be a troop for whom alone   135
One of my clearest moones I have put on,
A troope that lookes as if thy selfe and I
Had pluckt our reines in, and our whips laid by
To gaze upon these mortals, that appeare
Brighter then we.   140

NIGHT.   Then let us keepe 'em here,
And never more our chariots drive away,
But hold our places and out-shine the day.

CYNTHIA.   Great Queene of shaddowes you are pleasd to speake
    Of more then may be done, we may not breake   145
    The gods decrees, but when our time is come,
    Must drive away and give the day our roome.
    Yet whil'st our raigne lasts, let us stretch our power
    To give our servants one contented houre,
    With such unwonted solemne grace and state   150
    As may for ever after force them hate
    Our brothers glorious beames, and wish the night,
    Crown'd with a thousand starres, and our cold light:
    For almost all the world their service bend
    To *Phoebus*, and in vaine my light I lend,   155
    Gaz'd on unto my setting from my rise
    Almost of none, but of unquiet eyes.
NIGHT.   Then shine at full faire Queen, and by thy power
    Produce a birth to crowne this happy houre,
    Of Nimphes and shepheards, let their songs discover   160
    Easie and sweete who is a happy lover,
    Or if thou w'oot then call *Endimion*
    From the sweete flowrie bed he lies upon,
    On *Latmus* top, thy pale beames drawe away,
    And of this long night let him make thy day.   165
CYNTHIA.   Thou dreamst darke Queene, that faire boy was not mine,
    Nor went I downe to kisse him, ease and wine
    Have bred these bold tales, poets when they rage
    Turne gods to men, and make an houre an age,
    But I will give a greater state and glory,   170
    And raise to time a nobler memory
    Of what these lovers are: rise, rise, I say,
    Thou power of deepes, thy surges laid away,
    Neptune great King of waters, and by me
    Be proud to be commanded.   175

NEPTUNE *rises.*

NEPTUNE.   *Cinthia* see,
    Thy word hath fetcht me hither, let me know
    Why I ascend.
CYNTHIA.   Doth this majestick show
    Give thee no knowledge yet?   180

NEPTUNE.   Yes, now I see
   Something entended *Cinthia* worthy thee,
   Go on, ile be a helper.
CYNTHIA.   Hie thee then,
   And charge the winde goe from his rockie den,   185
   Let loose his subjects, onely *Boreas*
   Too foule for our intensions as he was,
   Still keepe him fast chain'd, we must have none here
   But vernall blasts and gentle winds appeare,
   Such as blow flowers, and through the glad bowes sing   190
   Many soft welcomes to the lusty spring.
   These are our musicke: next thy watrie race
   Bring on in couples, we are pleas'd to grace
   This noble night each in their richest things
   Your owne deepes or the broken vessell brings,   195
   Be prodigall and I shall be as kinde,
   And shine at full upon you.

Enter EOLUS *out of a Rock.*

NEPTUNE.   Oh, the winde commanding *Eolus.*
EOLUS.   Great *Neptune.*
NEPTUNE.   He.   200
EOLUS.   What is thy will?
NEPTUNE.   We doe command thee free
   Favonius and thy milder winds to waite
   Upon our *Cinthia*, but tie *Boreas* straight,
   Hee's too rebellious.   205
EOLUS.   I shall doe it.
NEPTUNE.   Doe.

                            ⟨*Exit* EOLUS.⟩

EOLUS.   ⟨*within*⟩ Great maister of the floud, and all below
   Thy full command has taken. O! the Maine
   Neptune.   210

    207–11 Doe . . . Here] Doe maister of the floud, and all below/Thy full command
has taken/EOL. O! The Maine/*Neptune.*/NEPT. Here Q1; Doe great maister of the
floud, . . . Heere Q2. *Both* Qq *are corrupt at this point. With some hesitation I adopt
Theobald's amended business and ascription of speeches. Neptune's command at line*
215 *indicates that Aeolus had departed once already on Neptune's business.*

Neptune.   Here.

⟨Enter Eolus.⟩

Eolus.   *Boreas* has broken his chaine,
    And strugling with the rest has got away.
Neptune.   Let him alone ile take him up at sea,
    He will not long be thence, goe once againe   215
    And call out of the bottomes of the Maine,
    Blew *Proteus*, and the rest, charge them put on
    Their greatest pearles and the most sparkling stone
    The beaten rock breeds, tell this night is done
    By me a solemne honor to the Moone,   220
    Flie like a full saile.
Eolus.   I am gone.   ⟨*Exit.*⟩
Cynthia.   Darke night
    Strike a full scilence, doe a thorow right
    To this great *Chorus*, that our musique may   225
    Touch high as heaven, and make the East breake day
    At mid-night.

                                        Musique.

⟨Enter Sea Gods.⟩   *Song.*

                Cinthia to thy power and thee
                    we obey,
                Joy to this great company,   230
                    and no day
                Come to steale this night away
                Till the rites of love are ended,
                And the lusty Bridegroome say,
                Welcome light of all befriended.   235
                Pace out you waterie powers below,
                    let your feete
                Like the gallies when they row
                    even beate.
                Let your unknowne measures set   240
                To the still winds, tell to all
                That gods are come immortal great
                To honour this great Nuptuall.

                            The Measure.

Second Song.
Hold back thy houres darke night till we have done,
 The day will come too soone,   245
Young Maydes will curse thee if thou steal'st away,
 And leav'st their blushes open to the day,
  Stay, stay, and hide
  the blushes of the Bride.
Stay gentle night, and with thy darkenesse cover 250
 the kisses of her lover.
Stay and confound her teares and her shrill cryings,
 Her weake denials, vowes and often dyings,
  Stay and hide all,
  but helpe not though she call.   255

NEPTUNE. Great Queene of us and heaven,
 Heare what I bring to make this houre a full one,
 If not her measure.
CYNTHIA. Speake Seas King.
NEPTUNE. The tunes my *Amphitrite* joyes to have, 260
 When they will dance upon the rising wave,
 And court me as the sayles, my *Tritons* play
 Musicke to lay a storme, Ile lead the way.

             Measure.

Song
To bed, to bed, come Hymen lead the Bride,
 And lay her by her husbands side: 265
 Bring in the virgins every one
 That greeve to lie alone;
That they may kisse, while they may say a maid,
To morrow t'will be other kist and said:
 Hesperus *be long a shining,*   270
 Whilst these lovers are a twining.

⟨*Enter* EOLUS.⟩
EOLUS. Ho *Neptune.*
NEPTUNE. *Eolus.*
EOLUS. The sea goes hie,

 263 lay] DYCE; lead Q2. *Almost certainly* Q2 *shows compositorial anticipation of the same word later in the line. It is inapt in context, since Boreas' storm follows.*

Boreas has rais'd a storme, goe and apply
Thy trident, else I prophesie, ere day,   275
Many a tall ship will be cast away;
Desend with all the gods, and all their powre
To strike a calme.
CYNTHIA. `A thankes to every one, and to gratulate   280
So great a service done at my desire,
Ye shall have many floods fuller and higher
Then you have wisht for, and no eb shall dare
To let the day see where your dwellings are.
Now back unto your governments in hast,   285
Least your proud charge should swell above the wast,
And win upon the Iland.
NEPTUNE.   We obey.

> NEPTUNE *descends, and the Sea Gods.*

CYNTHIA.   Hold up thy head dead night, seest thou not day?
The East begins to lighten, I must downe   290
And give my brother place.
NIGHT.   Oh I could frowne
To see the day, the day that flings his light
Upon my kingdomes, and contemnes olde night,
Let him goe on, and flame, I hope to see   295
Another wild fire in his axeltree,
And all fall drencht, but I forget, speake Queene,
The day growes on, I must no more be seene.
CYNTHIA.   Heave up thy drowsie head agen and see
A great light, a greater Majestie   300
Betweene our set and us, whip up thy teame
The day breaks here, and yon same flashing streame
Shot from the south, say, which way wilt thou goe?
NIGHT.   Ile vanish into mists.
CYNTHIA.   I into day. Adew.   305

> *Exeunt. Finis Maske.*

KING.   Take lights there Ladyes, get the Bride to bed,
We will not see you laid, good night *Amintor.*
Weele ease you of that tedious ceremony,
Were it my case I should thinke time runne slow:

If thou beest noble youth, get me a boy   310
That may defend my Kingdomes from my foes.
AMINTOR.   All happinesse to you.
KING.   Good night *Melantius*.

Exeunt.

ACT II

⟨SCENE I⟩

Enter EVADNE, ASPATIA, DULA, *and other Ladyes.*

DULA.   Madame shall we undresse you for this fight?
The wars are nak't that you must make to night.
EVADNE.   You are very merry *Dula*.
DULA.   I should be far merrier Madame, if it were with me
As it is with you.   5
EVADNE.   Howes that?
DULA.   That I might goe to bed with him with credit that you doe.
EVADNE.   Why how now wench?
DULA.   Come Ladyes will you helpe?
EVADNE.   I am soone undone.   10
DULA.   And as soone done,
Good store of clothes will trouble you at both.
EVADNE.   Art thou drunke *Dula*?
DULA.   Why heres none but we.
EVADNE.   Thou thinkst belike there is no modesty   15
When we'are alone.
DULA.   I by my troth, you hit my thoughts aright.
EVADNE.   You prick me Lady.
FIRST LADY.   Tis against my will.
DULA.   Anon you must indure more and lie still,   20
You're best to practise.
EVADNE.   Sure this wench is mad.
DULA.   No faith, this is a trick that I have had
Since I was foureteene.
EVADNE.   Tis high time to leave it.   25
DULA.   Nay now ile keepe it till the trick leave me,

    A dozen wanton words put in your head,
    Will make you livelier in your husbands bed.

EVADNE.   Nay faith then take it.

DULA.   Take it Madame, where?   30
    We all I hope will take it that are here.

EVADNE.   Nay then ile give you ore.

DULA.   So will I make
    The ablest man in *Rhodes* or his heart ake.

EVADNE.   Wilt take my place to night?   35

DULA.   Ile hold your cards against any two I know.

EVADNE.   What wilt thou doe?

DULA.   Madame weele doo't, and make'm leave play too.

EVADNE.   *Aspatia* take her part.

DULA.   I will refuse it.   40
    She will pluck downe a side, she does not use it.

EVADNE.   Why doe I prethee.

DULA.   You will finde the play
    Quickly, because your head lies well that way.

EVADNE.   I thanke thee Dula, would thou couldst instill   45
    Some of thy mirth into *Aspatia*:
    Nothing but sad thoughts in her brest doe dwell,
    Me thinkes a meane betwixt you would doe well.

DULA.   She is in love, hang me if I were so,
    But I could run my Countrey, I love too,   50
    To doe those things that people in love doe.

ASPATIA.   It were a timelesse smile should prove my cheeke,
    It were a fitter houre for me to laugh,
    When at the Alter the religious Priest,
    Were passifying the offended powers,   55
    With sacrifice, then now, this should have beene
    My right, and all your hands have bin imployd
    In giving me a spotlesse offering
    To young *Amintors* bed, as we are now
    For you: pardon *Evadne*, would my worth   60
    Were great as yours, or that the King, or he,

    II. I. 35 take] Q2; lie in Q1. Q1's *version loses the point for the wordplay which follows.*

    57 right] Q1; night Q2. *Either reading is possible, but the occurrence of* right/rite *elsewhere suggests that* Q2 *is a misreading.*

Or both thought so, perhaps he found me worthlesse,
But till he did so, in these eares of mine,
(These credulous eares) he powred the sweetest words
That art or love could frame, if he were false   65
Pardon it heaven, and if I did want
Vertue, you safely may forgive that too,
For I have lost none that I had from you.

EVADNE.   Nay leave this sad talke Madame.

ASPATIA.   Would I could, then I should leave the cause.   70

EVADNE.   See if you have not spoild all *Dulas* mirth.

ASPATIA.   Thou thinkst thy heart hard, but if thou beest caught
remember me; thou shalt perceive a fire shot suddenly into thee.

DULA.   Thats not so good, let 'em shoot any thing but fire, and
I feare 'm not.   75

ASPATIA.   Well wench thou maist be taken.

EVADNE.   Ladies good night, Ile doe the rest my selfe.

DULA.   Nay let your Lord doe some.

ASPATIA.   ⟨*sings*⟩ Lay a garland on my hearse of the dismall
Yew.

EVADNE.   Thats one of your sad songs Madame.   80

ASPATIA.   Beleeve me tis a very prety one.

EVADNE.   How is it Madame?

Song.

ASPATIA.   Lay a garland on my hearse of the dismall Yew,
Maidens willow branches beare, say I died true,
My love was false, but I was firme, from my houre of birth,   85
Upon my buried body lay lightly gentle earth.

EVADNE.   Fie ont Madame, the words are so strange, they are able
to make one dreame of hobgoblines. I could never have the power,
sing that *Dula*.

DULA.   ⟨*sings*⟩ I could never have the power
To love one above an houre,
But my heart would prompt mine eie
On some other man to flie,
Venus fix mine eies fast,
Or if not, give me all that I shall see at last.   95

EVADNE.   So leave me now.

DULA.   Nay we must see you laid.

ASPATIA.　Madame good night, may all the mariage joyes
　　That longing maides imagine in their beds
　　Prove so unto you, may no discontent　　　　　　　　100
　　Grow twixt your love and you, but if there doe,
　　Enquire of me and I will guide your mone,
　　And teach you an artificiall way to grieve,
　　To keepe your sorrow waking, love your Lord
　　No worse then I, but if you love so well,　　　　　105
　　Alas you may displease him, so did I,
　　This is the last time you shall looke on me:
　　Ladies farewell, as soone as I am dead,
　　Come all and watch one night about my hearse,
　　Bring each a mournefull storie and a teare,　　　110
　　To offer at it when I goe to earth;
　　With flattering Ivy claspe my coffin round,
　　Write on my brow my fortune, let my beere
　　Be borne by Virgins that shall sing by course
　　The truth of maides, and perjuries of men.　　　115
EVADNE.　Alas I pittie thee.

　　　　　　　　　　　　　　　　Exit EVADNE.

OMNES.　Madame good night.
FIRST LADY.　Come weele let in the Bridegroome.
DULA.　Where's my Lord?
FIRST LADY.　Here take this light.　　　　　　　120

Enter AMINTOR.

DULA.　You'le finde her in the darke.
FIRST LADY.　Your Ladye's scarse a bed yet, you must helpe her.
ASPATIA.　Goe and be happy in your Ladyes love,
　　May all the wrongs that you have done to me,
　　Be utterly forgotten in my death,　　　　　　　125
　　Ile trouble you no more, yet I will take
　　A parting kisse, and will not be denied.
　　You'le come my Lord and see the virgins weepe,
　　When I am laid in earth; though you your selfe
　　Can know no pittie: thus I winde my selfe　　　130
　　Into this willow garland, and am prouder
　　That I was once your love, (though now refus'd)

T.M.T.—2*

Then to have had another true to me.
So with praiers I leave you, and must trie
Some yet unpractis'd way to grieve and die.   135

Exit ASPATIA.

DULA.   Come Ladies will you goe.
OMNES.   Good night my Lord.
AMINTOR.   Much happinesse unto you all.

Exeunt Ladies.

I did that Lady wrong, me thinkes I feele
Her griefe shoot suddenly through all my veines,   140
Mine eyes runne, this is strange at such a time.
It was the King first mov'd me too't, but he
Has not my will in keeping, — why doe I
Perplex my selfe thus? something whispers me,
Goe not to bed, my guilt is not so great   145
As mine owne conscience (too sencible)
Would make me thinke, I onely brake a promise,
And twas the King that forst me: timerous flesh,
Why shakst thou so? away my idle feares.

Enter EVADNE.

Yonder is she, the luster of whose eie,   150
Can blot away the sad remembrance
Of all these things: oh my *Evadne* spare
That tender body, let it not take cold,
The vapors of the night will not fall here:
To bed my love, *Hymen* will punish us   155
For being slack performers of his rites.
Camst thou to call me?
EVADNE.   No.
AMINTOR.   Come, come, my love,
And let us loose our selves to one another,   160
Why art thou up so long?
EVADNE.   I am not well.
AMINTOR.   To bed, then let me winde thee in these armes,
Till I have banisht sicknesse.
EVADNE.   Good my Lord I cannot sleepe.   165

AMINTOR.   *Evadne* weele watch, I meane no sleeping.
EVADNE.   Ile not goe to bed.
AMINTOR.   I prethee doe.
EVADNE.   I will not for the world.
AMINTOR.   Why my deere love?   170
EVADNE.   Why? I have sworne I will not.
AMINTOR.   Sworne!
EVADNE.   I.
AMINTOR.   How sworne *Evadne*?
EVADNE.   Yes, sworne *Amintor*, and will sweare againe   175
   If you will wish to heare me.
AMINTOR.   To whom have you sworne this?
EVADNE.   If I should name him the matter were not great.
AMINTOR.   Come, this is but the coynesse of a bride.
EVADNE.   The coynesse of a bride?   180
AMINTOR.   How pretilie that frowne becomes thee.
EVADNE.   Doe you like it so?
AMINTOR.   Thou canst not dresse thy face in such a looke,
   But I shall like it.
EVADNE.   What looke likes you best?   185
AMINTOR.   Why doe you aske?
EVADNE.   That I may shew you one lesse pleasing to you.
AMINTOR.   Howes that?
EVADNE.   That I may shew you one lesse pleasing to you.
AMINTOR.   I prethee put thy jests in milder lookes,   190
   It shewes as thou wert angry.
EVADNE.   So perhaps I am indeede.
AMINTOR.   Why, who has done thee wrong?
   Name me the man, and by thy selfe I sweare,
   Thy yet unconquered selfe, I will revenge thee.   195
EVADNE.   Now I shall trie thy truth, if thou doest love me,
   Thou waighst not any thing compar'd with me,
   Life, honour, joyes eternall, all delights
   This world can yeeld, or hopefull people faine,
   Or in the life to come, are light as aire   200
   To a true lover when his Lady frownes,
   And bids him doe this: wilt thou kill this man?
   Sweare my *Amintor*, and ile kisse the sin
   Off from thy lips.

AMINTOR.   I wonnot swear sweet love, till I do know the cause. 205
EVADNE.   I wood thou wouldst,
   Why, it is thou that wrongst me, I hate thee,
   Thou should'st have kild thy selfe.
AMINTOR.   If I should know that, I should quickly kill
   The man you hated.   210
EVADNE.   Know it then and doo't.
AMINTOR.   Oh no, what looke so ere thou shalt put on,
   To trie my faith, I shall not thinke thee false,
   I cannot finde one blemish in thy face
   Where falsehood should abide, leave and to bed,   215
   If you have sworne to any of the virgins
   That were your olde companions to preserve
   Your maidenhead a night, it may be done
   Without this meanes.
EVADNE.   A maidenhead *Amintor* at my yeares?   220
AMINTOR.   Sure she raves, this cannot be
   Thy naturall temper, shall I call thy maides?
   Either thy healthfull sleepe hath left thee long,
   Or else some feaver rages in thy blood.
EVADNE.   Neither *Amintor* thinke you I am mad,   225
   Because I speake the truth?
AMINTOR.   Is this the truth, wil you not lie with me to night?
EVADNE.   To night? you talke as if you thought I would here-
   after.
AMINTOR.   Hereafter, yes I doe.
EVADNE.   You are deceiv'd, put off amazement, and with patience 230
   marke
   What I shall utter, for the Oracle
   Knowes nothing truer, tis not for a night
   Or two that I forbeare thy bed, but ever.
AMINTOR.   I dreame — awake *Amintor*.
EVADNE.   You heare right,   235
   I sooner will finde out the beds of Snakes,
   And with my youthfull blood warme their cold flesh,
   Letting them curle themselves about my limbes,
   Then sleepe one night with thee; this is not faind,
   Nor sounds it like the coynesse of a bride.   240
AMINTOR.   Is flesh so earthly to endure all this?

Are these the joyes of mariage? *Hymen* keepe
This story (that will make succeeding youth
Neglect thy ceremonies) from all eares.
Let it not rise up for thy shame and mine   245
To after ages, we will scorne thy lawes,
If thou no better blesse them, touch the heart
Of her that thou hast sent me, or the world
Shall know, there's not an altar that will smoake
In praise of thee, we will adopt us sonnes,   250
Then vertue shall inherit, and not blood:
If we doe lust, we'le take the next we meet,
Serving our selves as other creatures doe,
And never take note of the female more,
Nor of her issue. I doe rage in vaine,   255
She can but jest; Oh pardon me my love,
So deare the thoughts are which I hold of thee,
That I must breake forth; satisfie my feare:
It is a paine beyond the hand of death,
To be in doubt; confirme it with an oath,   260
If this be true.
EVADNE.   Doe you invent the forme,
    Let there be in it all the binding wordes
    Divels and conjurers can put together,
    And I will take it, I have sworne before,   265
    And here by all things holy doe againe,
    Never to be acquainted with thy bed.
    Is your doubt over now?
AMINTOR.   I know too much, would I had doubted still:
    Was ever such a mariage night as this?   270
    You powers above, if you did ever meane
    Man should be us'd thus, you have thought a way
    How he may beare himselfe, and save his honour:
    Instruct me in it, for to my dull eyes
    There is no meane, no moderate course to runne.   275
    I must live scorn'd, or be a murderer:
    Is there a third? why is this night so calme?
    Why does not heaven speake in thunder to us,
    And drowne her voyce?
EVADNE.   This rage will doe no good.   280

AMINTOR.   *Evadne*, heare me, thou hast tane an oath,
   But such a rash one, that to keepe it, were
   Worse then to sweare it, call it backe to thee,
   Such vowes as those never ascend the heaven,
   A teare or two will wash it quite away: 285
   Have mercy on my youth, my hopefull youth,
   If thou be pittifull, for (without boast)
   This land was proud of me: what Lady was there
   That men cald faire and vertuous in this Isle,
   That would have shund my love? It is in thee   290
   To make me hold this worth — Oh we vaine men
   That trust all our reputation
   To rest upon the weake and yeelding hand
   Of feeble woman: but thou art not stone;
   Thy flesh is soft, and in thine eyes doe dwell   295
   The spirit of love, thy heart cannot be hard,
   Come leade me from the bottome of dispaire,
   To all the joyes thou hast, I know thou wilt,
   And make me carefull least the sudden change
   Ore-come my spirits.   300
EVADNE.   When I call back this oath, the paines of hell inviron me.
AMINTOR.   I sleepe, and am to temporate, come to bed,
   Or by those haires, which if thou hast a soule like to thy locks,
   Were threads for Kings to weare
   About their armes—   305
EVADNE.   Why so perhaps they are.
AMINTOR.   Ile dragge thee to my bed, and make thy tongue
   Undoe this wicked oath, or on thy flesh
   Ile print a thousand wounds to let out life.
EVADNE.   I feare thee not, doe what thou darst to me,   310
   Every ill sounding word, or threatning looke
   Thou shewest to me, will be reveng'd at full.
AMINTOR.   It will not sure *Evadne*.
EVADNE.   Doe not you hazard that.
AMINTOR.   Ha ye your Champions?   315
EVADNE.   Alas *Amintor* thinkst thou I forbeare
   To sleepe with thee, because I have put on
   A maidens strictnesse? looke upon these cheekes,

And thou shalt finde the hot and rising blood
Unapt for such a vow, no, in this heart   320
There dwels as much desire, and as much will
To put that wished act in practise, as ever yet
Was knowne to woman, and they have been showne
Both, but it was the folly of thy youth,
To thinke this beauty (to what hand soe're   325
It shall be cald) shall stoope to any second.
I doe enjoy the best, and in that height
Have sworne to stand or die: you guesse the man.

AMINTOR.   No, let me know the man that wrongs me so:
That I may cut his body into motes,   330
And scatter it before the Northren winde.

EVADNE.   You dare not strike him.

AMINTOR.   Doe not wrong me so,
    Yes, if his body were a poysonous plant,
    That it were death to touch, I have a soule   335
    Will throw me on him.

EVADNE.   Why tis the King.

AMINTOR.   The King?

EVADNE.   What will you doe now?

AMINTOR.   Tis not the King.   340

EVADNE.   What did he make this match for, dull *Amintor?*

AMINTOR.   Oh thou hast nam'd a word that wipes away
    All thoughts revengefull, in that sacred name,
    The King, there lies a terror: what fraile man
    Dares lift his hand against it? let the Gods   345
    Speake to him when they please, till when let us
    Suffer, and waite.

EVADNE.   Why should you fill your selfe so full of heate,
    And haste so to my bed? I am no virgin.

AMINTOR.   What Divell hath put it in thy fancy then   350
    To mary mee?

EVADNE.   Alas, I must have one
    To father children, and to beare the name
    Of husband to me, that my sinne may be
    More honorable.   355

---

325 hand] DANIEL; land Qq. *Evadne compares herself to a hawk who will only fly to hand (stoop) at the summons of its royal master.*

AMINTOR.   What a strange thing am I?

EVADNE.   A miserable one, one that my selfe
  Am sory for.

AMINTOR.   Why shew it then in this,
  If thou hast pittie, though thy love be none,   360
  Kill me, and all true lovers that shall live
  In after ages crost in their desires,
  Shall blesse thy memorie, and call thee good,
  Because such mercy in thy heart was found,
  To rid a lingring wretch.   365

EVADNE.   I must have one
  To fill thy roome againe if thou wert dead,
  Else by this night I would: I pitty thee.

AMINTOR.   These strange and sudden injuries have falen
  So thick upon me, that I lose all sense   370
  Of what they are: me thinkes I am not wrong'd,
  Nor is it ought, if from the censuring world
  I can but hide it — reputation
  Thou art a word, no more, but thou hast showne
  An impudence so high, that to the world   375
  I feare thou wilt betray or shame thy selfe.

EVADNE.   To cover shame I tooke thee, never feare
  That I would blaze my selfe.

AMINTOR.   Nor let the King
  Know I conceive he wrongs me, then mine honour   380
  Will thrust me into action, that my flesh
  Could beare with patience, and it is some ease
  To me in these extreames, that I knew this
  Before I toucht thee; else had all the sinnes
  Of mankinde stood betwixt me and the King,   385
  I had gone through 'em to his hart and thine.
  I have lost one desire, tis not his crowne
  Shall buy me to thy bed: now I resolve
  He has dishonour'd thee, give me thy hand,
  Be carefull of thy credit, and sinne close,   390
  Tis all I wish, upon thy chamber floure
  Ile rest to night, that morning visiters
  May thinke we did as married people use,
  And prethee smile upon me when they come,

And seeme to toy as if thou hadst beene pleas'd   395
  With what we did.
EVADNE.   Feare not, I will doe this.
AMINTOR.   Come let us practise, and as wantonly
  As ever loving bride and bridegroome met,
  Lets laugh and enter here.   400
EVADNE.   I am content.
AMINTOR.   Downe all the swellings of my troubled heart.
  When we walke thus intwind let all eyes see
  If ever lovers better did agree.

                                        Exeunt.

                    ⟨ACT II⟩

                    ⟨SCENE II⟩

        Enter ASPATIA, ANTIPHILA, OLIMPIAS.

ASPATIA.   Away, you are not sad, force it no further,
  Good gods, how well you looke! such a full colour
  Young bashfull brides put on: sure you are new maried.
ANTIPHILA.   Yes Madame to your griefe.
ASPATIA.   Alas poore wentches.   5
  Goe learne to love first, learne to lose your selves,
  Learne to be flattered, and beleeve and blesse
  The double tongue that did it,
  Make a faith out of the miracles of ancient lovers,
  Such as speake truth and di'd in't,   10
  And like me beleeve all faithfull, and be miserable,
  Did you nere love yet wenches? speake *Olimpias*,
  Thou hast an easie temper, fit for stamp.
OLIMPIAS.   Never.
ASPATIA.   Nor you *Antiphila?*   15
ANTIPHILA.   Nor I.
ASPATIA.   Then my good girles be more then women, wise.
  At least, be more then I was, and bee sure
  You credit any thing the light gives life to,

II. II. 9–11 Make a faith ... miserable,] *om.* Q1. Q2 *misplaces lines* 9 *and* 10
after 11.

Before a man; rather beleeve the sea   20
Weepes for the ruin'd marchant when he rores,
Rather the wind but courts the pregnant sailes
When the strong cordage crackes, rather the sunne
Comes but to kisse the fruit in wealthy Autumme,
When all falles blasted; if you needs must love   25
(Forc'd by ill fate) take to your maiden bosomes
Two dead cold Aspicks, and of them make lovers,
They cannot flatter nor forsweare; one kisse
Makes a long peace for all; but man,
Oh that beast man: come lets be sad my girles,   30
That downe cast of thine eye *Olimpias*
Showes a fine sorrow; marke *Antiphila*,
Just such another was the Nymph *Oenones*
When *Paris* brought home *Hellen*, now a teare,
And then thou art a peece expressing fully   35
The *Carthage* Queene when from a cold Sea rock,
Full with her sorrow, she tyed fast her eyes,
To the faire *Trojan* ships, and having lost them,
Just as thine does, downe stole a teare *Antiphila*:
What would this wench doe if she were *Aspatia*?   40
Here she would stand, till some more pittying god
Turnd her to Marble: tis enough my wench,
Show me the peece of needle worke you wrought.
ANTIPHILA.   Of *Ariadne* Madame?
ASPATIA.   Yes that peece,   45
This should be *Theseus*, has a cousening face,
You ment him for a man.
ANTIPHILA.   He was so Madame.
ASPATIA.   Why then tis well enough, never looke backe,
You have a full winde, and a false heart *Theseus*,   50
Does not the story say, his Keele was split,
Or his masts spent, or some kind rock or other
Met with his vessell?
ANTIPHILA.   Not as I remember.
ASPATIA.   It should ha been so, could the Gods know this, 55
And not of all their number raise a storme,
But they are all as ill. This false smile was well exprest,
Just such another caught me, you shall not goe so:

Antiphila, in this place worke a quick-sand,
And over it a shallow smiling water,   60
And his ship plowing it, and then a feare.
Doe that feare to the life wench.
ANTIPHILA.   Twill wrong the storie.
ASPATIA.   Twill make the story wronged by wanton Poets,
Live long and be beleev'd; but wheres the Lady?   65
ANTIPHILA.   There Madame.
ASPATIA.   Fie, you have mist it heere *Antiphila*,
You are much mistaken wench:
These colours are not dull and pale enough,
To show a soule so full of miserie   70
As this sad Ladies was, doe it by me,
Doe it againe, by me the lost *Aspatia*,
And you shall find all true but the wild Iland,
And thinke I stand upon the sea breach now
Mine armes thus, and mine haire blowne with the wind,   75
Wilde as that desart, and let all about me
Tell that I am forsaken, doe my face
(If thou hadst ever feeling of a sorrow)
Thus, thus, *Antiphila* strive to make me looke
Like sorrowes monument, and the trees about me   80
Let them be dry and leavelesse, let the rocks
Groane with continuall surges, and behind me
Make all a desolation, looke, looke wenches,
A miserable life of this poore picture.
OLIMPIAS.   Deare Madame.   85
ASPATIA.   I have done, sit downe, and let us
Upon that point fixe all our eyes, that point there;
Make a dumbe silence till you feele a sudden sadnesse
Give us new soules.

Enter CALIANAX.

CALIANAX.   The King may doe this, and he may not doe it, 90
My childe is wrongd, disgrac'd: well, how now huswives?
What at your ease? is this a time to sit still? up you young
Lazie whores, up or ile swenge you.
OLIMPIAS.   Nay good my Lord.
CALIANAX.   You'l lie downe shortly, get you in and worke, 95

What are you growne so restie? you want heates,
We shall have some of the Court boyes doe that office.
ANTIPHILA.　My Lord we doe no more then we are charg'd:
　It is the Ladies pleasure we be thus in griefe,
　She is forsaken.　　　　　　　　　　　　　　　　　　100
CALIANAX.　Theres a rogue too,
　A young dissembling slave, well, get you in,
　Ile have a bout with that boy, tis hie time
　Now to be valiant, I confesse my youth
　Was never prone that way: what made an asse?　　105
　A Court stale? well I will be valiant,
　And beate some dozen of these whelps, and theres
　Another of 'em, a trim cheating souldier,
　Ile maule that raschall, has out-brav'd me twice,
　But now I thanke the Gods I am valiant,　　　　110
　Goe, get you in, ile take a course with all.

　　　　　　　　　　　　　　　　Exeunt omnes.

ACT III

⟨SCENE I⟩

Enter CLEON, STRATO, DIPHILUS.

CLEON.　Your sister is not up yet.
DIPHILUS.　Oh brides must take their mornings rest,
　The night is troublesome.
STRATO.　But not tedious.
DIPHILUS.　What ods, hee has not my sisters maiden-head to　5
　night?
STRATO.　None, its ods against any bridegrome living, he nere
　gets it while he lives.
DIPHILUS.　Y'are merry with my sister, you'le please to allow me
　the same freedome with your mother.
STRATO.　Shees at your service.　　　　　　　　　　10
DIPHILUS.　Then shees merry enough of herselfe, shee needs no
　tickling, knock at the dore.

　　　　　96 restie] rustie Q1; reasty Q2.

STRATO.   We shall interrupt them.

DIPHILUS.   No matter, they have the yeare before them, good
  morrow sister, spare your selfe to day, the night will come againe.   15

Enter AMINTOR.

AMINTOR.   Whose there, my brother? I am no readier yet, your
  sister is but now up.

DIPHILUS.   You looke as you had lost your eyes to night, I thinke
  you ha not slept.

AMINTOR.   Ifaith I have not.   20

DIPHILUS.   You have done better then.

AMINTOR.   We ventured for a boy, when hee is twelve,
  A shall command against the foes of *Rhodes*,
  Shall we be merry?

STRATO.   You cannot, you want sleepe.   25

AMINTOR.   [*aside.*] Tis true, but she
  As if she had drunke *Lethe*, or had made
  Even with heaven, did fetch so still a sleepe,
  So sweet and sound.

DIPHILUS.   Whats that?   30

AMINTOR.   Your sister frets this morning, and doth turne
  Her eyes upon mee, as people on their headsman,
  She does chafe, and kisse and chafe againe,
  And clap my cheeks, shees in another world.

DIPHILUS.   Then I had lost, I was about to lay,   35
  You had not got her maidenhead to night.

AMINTOR.   Ha, does hee not mocke mee, y'ad lost indeed,
  I doe not use to bungle.

CLEON.   You doe deserve her.

AMINTOR.   [*aside.*] I laid my lips to hers, and that wild breath   40
  That was so rude and rough to me, last night
  Was sweete as Aprill, ile be guilty too,
  If these be the effects.

Enter MELANTIUS.

MELANTIUS.   Good day *Amintor*, for to me the name
  Of brother is too distant, we are friends,   45
  And that is nearer.

AMINTOR.   Deare *Melantius*.
  Let me behold thee, is it possible?
MELANTIUS.   What sudden gaze is this?
AMINTOR.   Tis wondrous strange.   50
MELANTIUS.   Why does thine eye desire so strict a view
  Of that it knowes so well? theres nothing here
  That is not thine.
AMINTOR.   I wonder much *Melantius*,
  To see those noble lookes that make me thinke   55
  How vertuous thou art, and on the sudden
  Tis strange to me, thou shouldst have worth and honour,
  Or not be base and false, and treacherous,
  And every ill. But
MELANTIUS.   Stay, stay my friend,   60
  I feare this sound will not become our loves,
  No more embrace me.
AMINTOR.   Oh mistake me not,
  I know thee to be full of all those deeds,
  That we fraile men call good, but by the course   65
  Of nature thou shouldst be as quickly chang'd,
  As are the windes, dissembling, as the Sea,
  That now weares browes as smooth as virgins be,
  Tempting the Merchant to invade his face,
  And in an houre cals his billowes up,   70
  And shoots em at the Sun, destroying all
  A carries on him. [*aside.*] Oh how neare am I
  To utter my sicke thoughts.
MELANTIUS.   But why, my friend, should I be so by nature?
AMINTOR.   I have wed thy sister, who hath vertuous thoughts   75
  Enow for one whole familie, and it is strange
  That you should feele no want.
MELANTIUS.   Beleeve me this is complement too cunning for me.
DIPHILUS.   What should I be then by the course of nature,
  They having both robd me of so much vertue.   80
STRATO.   Oh call the bride, my Lord *Amintor*, that wee may see
  her blush, and turne her eyes downe, it is the pritiest sport.
AMINTOR.   *Evadne*.
EVADNE.   [*within.*] My Lord.
AMINTOR.   Come forth my love,   85

Your brothers doe attend, to wish you joy.

EVADNE.   I am not ready yet.

AMINTOR.   Enough, enough.

EVADNE.   They'le mocke me.

AMINTOR.   Faith thou shalt come in.   90

Enter EVADNE.

MELANTIUS.   Good morrow sister, he that understands
  Whom you have wed, need not to wish you joy.
  You have enough, take heed you be not proud.

DIPHILUS.   O sister what have you done?

EVADNE.   I done? why what have I done?   95

STRATO.   My Lord *Amintor* sweares you are no maid now.

EVADNE.   Push.

STRATO.   Ifaith he does.

EVADNE.   I knew I should be mockt.

DIPHILUS.   With a truth.   100

EVADNE.   If twere to do againe, in faith I would not mary.

AMINTOR.   [*aside.*] Nor I by heaven.

DIPHILUS.   Sister, *Dula* sweares she heard you cry two roomes off.

EVADNE.   Fie how you talke.

DIPHILUS.   Lets see you walke, *Evadne.* By my troth y'are spoild. 105

MELANTIUS.   *Amintor.*

AMINTOR.   Ha.

MELANTIUS.   Thou art sad.

AMINTOR.   Who I? I thanke you for that, shall *Diphilus* thou and
  I sing a catch?   110

MELANTIUS.   How?

AMINTOR.   Prethee lets.

MELANTIUS.   Nay thats too much the other way.

AMINTOR.   I am so lightned with my happinesse, how dost thou
  love? kisse me.   115

EVADNE.   I connot love you, you tell tales of me.

AMINTOR.   Nothing but what becomes us: Gentlemen,

III. I. 105 DIPHILUS. Lets see you walke, *Evadne.* By my troth y'are spoild.]
THEOBALD; *Diph.* Lets see you walke./*Evad.* By my troth y'are spoild.
91-2. Spoild, *i.e. despoiled, is more pertinent applying to Evadne than to Diphilus.*
O.E.D. does not record anything approaching the spoilt child sense of the term before
1648.

Would you had all such wives, and all the world,
That I might be no wonder, y'are all sad;
What doe you envie me? I walke me thinkes   120
On water, and nere sinke I am so light.

MELANTIUS.   Tis well you are so.

AMINTOR.   Well? how can I be other when shee lookes thus?
Is there no musike there? lets dance.

MELANTIUS.   Why? this is strange, *Amintor*.   125

AMINTOR.   I do not know my selfe, [*aside*.] yet I could wish my
joy were lesse.

DIPHILUS.   Ile marrie too if it will make one thus.

EVADNE.   *Amintor*, harke.

AMINTOR.   What sayes my love? I must obey.

EVADNE.   You doe it scurvily, twill be perceiv'd.   130

CLEON.   My Lord the King is here.

Enter KING *and* LISIPPUS.

AMINTOR.   Where?

STRATO.   And his brother.

KING.   Good morrow all.
Amintor joy on joy fall thicke upon thee,   135
And Madame you are alterd since I saw you,
I must salute you, you are now anothers,
How lik't you your nights rest?

EVADNE.   Ill sir.

AMINTOR.   Indeede she tooke but little.   140

LISIPPUS.   You'le let her take more, and thanke her too shortly.

KING.   *Amintor* wert thou truely honest till thou wert married?

AMINTOR.   Yes sir.

KING.   Tell me then, how shewes the sport unto thee?

AMINTOR.   Why well.   145

KING.   What did you doe?

AMINTOR.   No more nor lesse then other couples use,
You know what tis, it has but a course name.

KING.   But prethee, I should thinke by her black eie
And her red cheeke, she should be quick and stirring   150
In this same businesse; ha?

AMINTOR.   I cannot tell, I nere tried other sir, but I perceive
She is as quick as you delivered.

KING.   Well youle trust me then *Amintor*.
   To choose a wife for you agen.   155
AMINTOR.   No never sir.
KING.   Why? like you this so ill?
AMINTOR.   So well I like her,
   For this I bow my knee in thanks to you,
   And unto heaven will pay my gratefull tribute   160
   Hourely, and doe hope we shall draw out
   A long contented life together here,
   And die both full of gray haires in one day,
   For which the thanks is yours, but if the powers
   That rule us, please to call her first away,   165
   Without pride spoke, this world holds not a wife
   Worthy to take her roome.
KING.   [*Aside.*] I doe not like this; all forbeare the roome
   But you *Amintor* and your Lady, I have some speech with you
   That may concerne your after living well.   170

⟨*Exeunt all but* KING, AMINTOR, EVADNE.⟩

AMINTOR.   A will not tell me that he lies with her; if hee doe,
   Something heavenly stay my heart, for I shall be apt
   To thrust this arme of mine to acts unlawfull.
KING.   You will suffer me to talke with her *Amintor*,
   And not have a jealous pang.   175
AMINTOR.   Sir, I dare trust my wife
   With whom she dares to talke, and not be jealous.
KING.   How doe you like *Amintor*?
EVADNE.   As I did sir.
KING.   Howes that?   180
EVADNE.   As one that to fulfill your will and pleasure,
   I have given leave to call me wife and love.
KING.   I see there is no lasting faith in sin,
   They that breake word with heaven, will breake agen
   With all the world, and so doest thou with me.   185
EVADNE.   How sir?
KING.   This subtle womans ignorance
   Will not excuse you, thou hast taken oathes
   So great, that me thought they did misbecome

  A womans mouth, that thou wouldst nere injoy   190
  A man but me.
EVADNE. I never did sweare so, you doe me wrong.
KING. Day and night have heard it.
EVADNE. I swore indeede that I would never love
  A man of lower place, but if your fortune   195
  Should throw you from this hight, I bad you trust
  I would forsake you, and would bend to him
  That won your throne, I love with my ambition,
  Not with my eies, but if I ever yet
  Toucht any other, Leprosie light here   200
  Upon my face, which for your royaltie
  I would not staine.
KING. Why thou dissemblest, and it is in me
  To punish thee.
EVADNE. Why, it is in me then, not to love you, which will 205
  More afflict your bodie, then your punishment can mine.
KING. But thou hast let *Amintor* lie with thee.
EVADNE. I hannot.
KING. Impudence, he saies himselfe so.
EVADNE. A lies.   210
KING. A does not.
EVADNE. By this light he does, strangely and basely, and
  Ile proove it so, I did not onely shun him for a night,
  But told him, I would never close with him.
KING. Speake lower, tis false.   215
EVADNE. I am no man to answer with a blow,
  Or if I were, you are the King, but urge not, tis most true.
KING. Doe not I know the uncontrouled thoughts,
  That youth brings with him, when his blood is high,
  With expectation and desire of that   220
  He long hath waited for? is not his spirit
  Though he be temperate, of a valiant straine,
  As this our age hath knowne? what could he doe
  If such a suddaine speech had met his blood,
  But ruine thee for ever? if he had not kild thee, 225
  He could not beare it thus, he is as we
  Or any other wrong'd man.
EVADNE. It is dissembling.

KING.   Take him, farewell, henceforth I am thy foe,
　　And what disgraces I can blot thee with, looke for.　　　　230
EVADNE.   Stay sir; *Amintor*, you shall heare *Amintor*.
AMINTOR.   What my love?
EVADNE.   *Amintor*, thou hast an ingenious looke,
　　And should'st be vertuous, it amazeth me
　　That thou can'st make such base malicious lies.　　　　235
AMINTOR.   What my deere wife?
EVADNE.   Deere wife? I doe despise thee,
　　Why nothing can be baser then to sow
　　Discention amongst lovers.
AMINTOR.   Lovers? who?　　　　240
EVADNE.   The King and me.
AMINTOR.   Oh God.
EVADNE.   Who should live long and love without distast
　　Were it not for such pickthanks as thy selfe.
　　Did you lie with me? sweare now, and be punisht in hell　　245
　　For this.
AMINTOR.   The faithlesse sin I made
　　To faire *Aspatia*, is not yet reveng'd,
　　It followes me, I will not loose a word
　　To this wilde woman, but to you my King　　　　250
　　The anguish of my soule thrusts out this truth.
　　Y'are a tirant, and not so much to wrong
　　An honest man thus, as to take a pride
　　In talking with him of it.
EVADNE.   Now sir, see how loud this fellow lied.　　　　255
AMINTOR.   You that can know to wrong, shold know how
　　Men must right themselves: what punishment is due
　　From me to him that shall abuse my bed?
　　It is not death, nor can that satisfie,
　　Unlesse I send your lives through all the land　　　　260
　　To show how nobly I have freed my selfe.
KING.   Draw not thy sword, thou knowst I cannot feare
　　A subjects hand, but thou shalt feele the weight
　　Of this if thou doest rage.
AMINTOR.   The weight of that?　　　　265
　　If you have any worth, for heavens sake thinke
　　I feare not swords, for as you are meere man,

I dare as easily kill you for this deede,
As you dare thinke to doe it: but there is
Divinitie about you, that strikes dead   270
My rising passions; as you are my King
I fall before you and present my sword,
To cut mine owne flesh if it be your will,
Alas! I am nothing but a multitude of
Waking griefes, yet should I murder you,   275
I might before the world take the excuse
Of madnesse, for compare my injuries,
And they will well appeare too sad a weight
For reason to endure, but fall I first
Amongst my sorrowes, ere my treacherous hand   280
Touch holy things, but why? I know not what
I have to say, why did you choose out me
To make thus wretched? there were thousands fooles
Easie to worke on, and of state enough
Within the Iland.   285

EVADNE.   I wold not have a foole, it were no credit for me.

AMINTOR.   Worse and worse:
Thou that darst talke unto thy husband thus,
Professe thy selfe a whore, and more then so,
Resolve to be so still, it is my fate   290
To beare and bow beneath a thousand griefes,
To keepe that little credit with the world,
But there were wise ones to: you might have tane another.

KING.   No, for I beleevd thee honest, as thou wert valiant.

AMINTOR.   All the happinesse   295
Bestowd upon me turnes into disgrace,
Gods take your honesty againe, for I
Am loaden with it, good my Lord the King
Be private in it.

KING.   Thou maist live *Amintor*,   300
Free as thy King, if thou wilt winke at this,
And be a meanes that we may meet in secret.

AMINTOR.   A baud, hold, hold my breast, a bitter curse
Ceaze me, if I forget not all respects
That are religious, on another word   305
Sounded like that, and through a Sea of sinnes

Will wade to my revenge, though I should call
Paines here, and after life, upon my soule.
KING.   Well, I am resolute, you lay not with her,
And so I leave you. 310

Exit KING.

EVADNE.   You must needs be prating, and see what follows.
AMINTOR.   Prethee vex me not,
Leave me, I am afraid some sudden start
Will pull a murther on me.
EVADNE.   I am gone, I love my life well. 315

Exit EVADNE.

AMINTOR.   I hate mine as much.
This tis to breake a troth, I should be glad,
If all this tide of griefe would make me mad.

Exit.

⟨ACT III⟩

⟨SCENE II⟩

Enter MELANTIUS.

MELANTIUS.   Ile know the cause of all *Amintors* griefes,
Or friendship shall be idle.

Enter CALIANAX.

CALIANAX.   O *Melantius*, my daughter will die.
MELANTIUS.   Trust me I am sory, would thou hadst tane her
roome.
CALIANAX.   Thou art a slave, a cut-throat slave, a bloody 5
treacherous slave.
MELANTIUS.   Take heed old man, thou wilt be heard to rave,
And lose thine offices.
CALIANAX.   I am valiant growne,
At all these yeares, and thou art but a slave.

309 lay not with] Q2; lay with Q1. *The word* resolute *is open to contrary interpreta-
tions, depending on the presence or absence of the negative in the line. The context
demands a negative, and therefore the sense* convinced *for* resolute.

MELANTIUS.   Leave, some companie will come, and I respect   10
    Thy yeares, not thee so much, that I could wish
    To laugh at thee alone.
CALIANAX.   Ile spoile your mirth, I meane to fight with thee,
    There lie my cloake, this was my fathers sword,
    And he durst fight, are you prepar'd?   15
MELANTIUS.   Why? wilt thou doate thy selfe
    Out of thy life? hence get thee to bed,
    Have carefull looking to, and eate warme things,
    And trouble not mee: my head is full of thoughts
    More waighty then thy life or death can be.   20
CALIANAX.   You have a name in warre, where you stand safe
    Amongst a multitude, but I will try
    What you dare doe unto a weake old man
    In single fight, you'l give ground I feare:
    Come draw.   25
MELANTIUS.   I will not draw, unlesse thou pulst thy death
    Upon thee with a stroke, theres no one blow
    That thou canst give, hath strength enough to kill me.
    Tempt me not so far then, the power of earth
    Shall not redeeme thee.   30
CALIANAX.   ⟨aside.⟩ I must let him alone,
    Hees stout, and able, and to say the truth,
    How ever I may set a face and talke,
    I am not valiant: when I was a youth
    I kept my credit with a testie tricke,   35
    I had mongst cowards, but durst never fight.
MELANTIUS.   I will not promise to preserve your life if you doe
    stay.
CALIANAX.   ⟨aside.⟩ I would give halfe my land that I durst fight
    with that proud man a little: if I had men to holde him, I would
    beate him, till hee aske mee mercie.   40
MELANTIUS.   Sir will you be gone?
CALIANAX.   ⟨aside.⟩ I dare not stay, but I will goe home and
    beate my servants all over for this.

                                               Exit CALIANAX.

MELANTIUS.   This old fellow haunts me,
    But the distracted carriage of mine *Amintor*   45

Takes deeply on me, I will find the cause,
I feare his conscience cries, he wronged *Aspatia*.

Enter AMINTOR.

AMINTOR.   Mens eyes are not so subtile to perceive
My inward miserie, I beare my griefe
Hid from the world, how art thou wretched then?   50
For ought I know all husbands are like me,
And every one I talke with of his wife,
Is but a well dissembler of his woes
As I am, would I knew it, for the rarenesse
Afflicts me now.   55
MELANTIUS.   *Amintor*, we have not enjoy'd our friendship of late,
For we were wont to charge our soules in talke.
AMINTOR.   *Melantius*, I can tell the a good jest of *Strato* and a
Lady the last day.
MELANTIUS.   How wast?   60
AMINTOR.   Why such an odde one.
MELANTIUS.   I have longd to speake with you, not of an idle jest
thats forst, but of matter you are bound to utter to me.
AMINTOR.   What is that my friend?
MELANTIUS.   I have observ'd, your wordes fall from your tongue   65
Wildely, and all your carriage
Like one that strove to shew his merry moode,
When he were ill dispos'd: you were not wont
To put such scorne into your speech, or weare
Upon your face ridiculous jollity: 70
Some sadnesse sits heere, which your cunning would
Cover ore with smiles, and twill not be;
What is it?
AMINTOR.   A sadnesse here? what cause
Can Fate provide for me to make me so?   75
Am I not lov'd through all this Isle? the King
Raines greatnesse on me: have I not received
A Lady to my bed, that in her eye
Keepes mounting fire, and on her tender cheekes
Inevitable colour, in her heart   80
A prison for all vertue, are not you,
Which is above all joyes, my constant friend?

What saddnesse can I have? no, I am light,
And feele the courses of my blood more warme
And stirring then they were; faith marry too,   85
And you will feele so unexprest a joy
In chaste embraces, that you will indeed
Appeare another.

MELANTIUS.   You may shape, *Amintor*,
Causes to cozen the whole world withall,   90
And your selfe too, but tis not like a friend,
To hide your soule from me: tis not your nature
To be thus idle, I have seene you stand
As you were blasted, midst of all your mirth,
Call thrice aloud, and then start, fayning joy   95
So coldly: world! what doe I here? a friend
Is nothing: heaven! I would ha told that man
My secret sinnes, ile search an unknowne land,
And there plant friendship, all is withered here,
Come with a complement, I would have fought,   100
Or told my friend a lied, ere soothd him so;
Out of my bosome.

AMINTOR.   But there is nothing.

MELANTIUS.   Worse and worse, farewell;
From this time have acquaintance, but no friend.   105

AMINTOR.   *Melantius*, stay, you shall know what that is.

MELANTIUS.   See how you plaid with friendship, be advis'd
How you give cause unto your selfe to say,
You ha lost a friend.

AMINTOR.   Forgive what I ha done,   110
For I am so ore-gon with injuries
Unheard of, that I lose consideration
Of what I ought to do, — oh — oh.

MELANTIUS.   Doe not weepe, what ist?
May I once but know the man   115
Hath turnd my friend thus.

AMINTOR.   I had spoke at first, but that —

MELANTIUS.   But what?

AMINTOR.   I held it most unfit
For you to know, faith doe not know it yet.   120

MELANTIUS.   Thou seest my love, that will keep company

With thee in teares, hide nothing then from me,
For when I know the cause of thy distemper,
With mine old armour ile adorne my selfe,
My resolution, and cut through thy foes,   125
Unto thy quiet, till I place thy heart
As peaceable as spotlesse innocence.
What is it?

AMINTOR.   Why tis this, — it is too bigge
   To get out, let my teares make way awhile.   130

MELANTIUS.   Punish me strangly heaven, if he scape
   Of life or fame, that brought this youth to this.

AMINTOR.   Your sister.

MELANTIUS.   Well sayd.

AMINTOR.   You'l wisht unknowne when you have heard it.   135

MELANTIUS.   No.

AMINTOR.   Is much to blame,
   And to the King has given her honour up,
   And lives in whoredome with him.

MELANTIUS.   How's this?   140
   Thou art run mad with injury indeed,
   Thou couldst not utter this else, speake againe,
   For I forgive it freely, tell thy griefes.

AMINTOR.   Shees wanton, I am loth to say a whore,
   Though it be true.   145

MELANTIUS.   Speake yet againe, before mine anger grow
   Up beyond throwing downe, what are thy griefes?

AMINTOR.   By all our friendship, these.

MELANTIUS.   What? am I tame?
   After mine actions, shall the name of friend   150
   Blot all our family, and strike the brand
   Of whore upon my sister unreveng'd?
   My shaking flesh be thou a witnesse for me,
   With what unwillingnesse I goe to scourge
   This rayler, whom my folly hath cald friend;   155
   I will not take thee basely, thy sword
   Hangs neere thy hand, draw it, that I may whip
   Thy rashnesse to repentance, draw thy sword.

AMINTOR.   Not on thee, did thine anger goe as high
   As troubled waters: thou shouldst doe me ease,   160

Heere, and eternally, if thy noble hand
Would cut me from my sorrowes.
MELANTIUS.   This is base,
  And fearefull, they that use to utter lies,
  Provide not blowes, but wordes to qualifie   165
  The men they wrong'd, thou hast a guilty cause.
AMINTOR.   Thou pleasest me, for so much more like this,
  Will raise my anger up above my griefes,
  Which is a passion easier to be borne,
  And I shall then be happy.   170
MELANTIUS.   Take then more, to raise thine anger. Tis meere
  Cowardise makes thee not draw, and I will leave thee dead
  How ever, but if thou art so much prest
  With guilt and feare, as not to dare to fight,
  Ile make thy memory loath'd and fix a scandall   175
  Upon thy name for ever.
AMINTOR.   Then I draw,
  As justly as our Magistrates their swords
  To cut offenders off; I knew before
  Twould grate your eares, but it was base in you   180
  To urge a waighty secret from your friend,
  And then rage at it, I shall be at ease
  If I be kild, and if you fall by me,
  I shall not long out live you.
MELANTIUS.   Stay a while,   185
  The name of friend is more then familie,
  Or all the world besides; I was a foole.
  Thou searching humane nature, that didst wake
  To doe me wrong, thou art inquisitive,
  And thrusts me upon questions that will take   190
  My sleepe away, would I had died ere knowne
  This sad dishonor, pardon me my friend,
  If thou wilt strike, here is a faithfull heart,
  Pearce it, for I will never heave my hand
  To thine, behold the power thou hast in me,   195
  I doe beleeve my sister is a whore,
  A leprous one, put up thy sword young man.
AMINTOR.   How should I beare it then she being so?
  I feare my friend that you will loose me shortly,

And I shall doe a foule act on my selfe   200
  Through these disgraces.
MELANTIUS.   Better halfe the land
  Were buried quick together, no, *Amintor*,
  Thou shalt have ease: Oh this adulterous King
  That drew her too't, where got he the spirit   205
  To wrong me so?
AMINTOR.   What is it then to me,
  If it be wrong to you?
MELANTIUS.   Why not so much: the credit of our house
  Is throwne away,   210
  But from his iron den ile waken death,
  And hurle him on this King, my honestie
  Shall steele my sword, and on my horrid point
  Ile weare my cause, that shall amaze the eyes
  Of this proud man, and be to glittring   215
  For him to looke on.
AMINTOR.   I have quite undone my fame.
MELANTIUS.   Drie up thy watrie eyes,
  And cast a manly looke upon my face,
  For nothing is so wilde as I thy friend   250
  Till I have freed thee, still this swelling brest,
  I goe thus from thee, and will never cease
  My vengeance till I finde thy heart at peace.
AMINTOR.   It must not be so, stay, mine eyes would tell
  How loath I am to this, but love and teares   225
  Leave me a while, for I have hazarded
  All that this world calls happy, thou hast wrought
  A secret from me under name of friend,
  Which art could nere have found, nor torture wrung
  From out my bosome, give it me agen,   230
  For I will finde it where so ere it lies
  Hid in the mortal'st part, invent a way
  To give it backe.
MELANTIUS.   Why would you have it backe?
  I will to death persue him with revenge.   235
AMINTOR.   Therefore I call it from thee, for I know
  Thy blood so high, that thou wilt stir in this,
  And shame me to posterity: take to thy weapon.

MELANTIUS.   Heare thy friend, that bears more yeares then thou.

AMINTOR.   I will not heare: but draw, or I—   240

MELANTIUS.   *Amintor.*

AMINTOR.   Draw then, for I am full as resolute
   As fame and honor can inforce me be,
   I cannot linger, draw.

MELANTIUS.   I doe — but is not   245
   My share of credit equall with thine,
   If I doe stir?

AMINTOR.   No; for it will be cald
   Honor in thee to spill thy sisters blood,
   If she her birth abuse, and on the King   250
   A brave revenge: but on me that have walkt
   With patience in it, it will fixe the name
   Of fearefull cuckold, — O that word!
   Be quick.

MELANTIUS.   Then joyne with me.   255

AMINTOR.   I dare not doe a sinne, or else I would: be
   speedy.

MELANTIUS.   Then dare not fight with me, for that's a sin.
   His griefe distracts him, call thy thoughts agen,
   And to thy selfe pronounce the name of friend,
   And see what that will worke, I will not fight.   260

AMINTOR.   You must.

MELANTIUS.   I will be kild first, though my passions
   Offered the like to you, tis not this earth
   Shall buy my reason to it, thinke a while,
   For you are (I must weepe when I speake that)   265
   All most besides your selfe.

AMINTOR.   Oh my soft temper,
   So many sweete words from thy sisters mouth,
   I am afraid would make me take her,
   To embrace and pardon her, I am mad indeede,   270
   And know not what I doe, yet have a care
   Of me in what thou doest.

MELANTIUS.   Why thinks my friend I will forget his honor, or to
   save
   The braverie of our house, will loose his fame,
   And feare to touch the throne of Majestie?   275

AMINTOR.   A curse will follow that, but rather live
    And suffer with me.
MELANTIUS.   I will doe what worth shall bid me, and no more.
AMINTOR.   Faith I am sicke, and desperately I hope,
    Yet leaning thus I feele a kinde of ease.   280
MELANTIUS.   Come take agen your mirth about you.
AMINTOR.   I shall never doo't.
MELANTIUS.   I warrant you, looke up, weele walke together,
    Put thine arme here, all shall be well agen.
AMINTOR.   Thy love, o wretched, I thy love *Melantius*, why   285
    I have nothing else.
MELANTIUS.   Be merry then.

                                                        Exeunt.

Enter MELANTIUS *agen.*

MELANTIUS.   This worthie yong man may doe violence
    Upon himselfe, but I have cherisht him
    As well as I could, and sent him smiling from me   290
    To counterfeit againe, sword hold thine edge,
    My heart will never faile me: *Diphilus,*

Enter DIPHILUS.

    Thou comst as sent.
DIPHILUS.   Yonder has bin such laughing.
MELANTIUS.   Betwixt whom?   295
DIPHILUS.   Why our sister and the King,
    I thought their spleenes would breake,
    They laught us all out of the roome.
MELANTIUS.   They must weepe *Diphilus.*
DIPHILUS.   Must they?   300
MELANTIUS.   They must: thou art my brother, and if I did beleeve
    Thou hadst a base thought, I would rip it out,
    Lie where it durst.
DIPHILUS.   You should not, I would first mangle my selfe and
        finde it.
MELANTIUS.   That was spoke according to our strain, come,
    Joyne thy hands to mine,   305
    And sweare a firmenesse to what project I
    Shall lay before thee.
DIPHILUS.   You doe wrong us both,

People hereafter shall not say there past
A bond more then our loves to tie our lives   310
And deathes together.
MELANTIUS.   It is as nobly said as I would wish,
Anon ile tell you wonders, we are wrong'd.
DIPHILUS.   But I will tell you now, weele right our selves.
MELANTIUS.   Stay not, prepare the armour in my house,   315
And what friends you can draw unto our side,
Not knowing of the cause, make ready too,
Hast *Diphilus* the time requires it, hast.

Exit DIPHILUS.

I hope my cause is just, I know my blood
Tels me it is, and I will credit it: 320
To take revenge and loose my selfe withall,
Were idle, and to scape, impossible,
Without I had the fort, which miserie
Remaining in the hands of my olde enemy
Calianax, but I must have it, see   325

Enter CALIANAX.

Where he comes shaking by me, good my Lord
Forget your spleene to me, I never wrong'd you,
But would have peace with every man.
CALIANAX.   Tis well:
If I durst fight, your tongue would lie at quiet.   330
MELANTIUS.   Y'are touchie without all cause.
CALIANAX.   Doe, mock me.
MELANTIUS.   By mine honor I speake truth.
CALIANAX.   Honor? where ist?
MELANTIUS.   See what starts you make into your hatred   335
To my love and freedome to you.
I come with resolution to obtaine a sute
Of you.
CALIANAX.   A sute of me? tis very like it should be granted sir.
MELANTIUS.   Nay, goe not hence,   340
Tis this, you have the keeping of the fort,
And I would wish you by the love you ought

　　　To beare unto me, to deliver it
　　　Into my hands.

CALIANAX.　I am in hope thou art mad, to talke to me thus.　345

MELANTIUS.　But there is a reason to move you to it, I would
　　　Kill the King, that wrong'd you and your daughter.

CALIANAX.　Out traitor.

MELANTIUS.　Nay but stay, I cannot scape, the deede once done,
　　　Without I have this fort.　350

CALIANAX.　And should I help thee? now thy treacherous mind
　　　Betraies it selfe.

MELANTIUS.　Come delay me not,
　　　Give me a suddaine answere, or already
　　　Thy last is spoke, refuse not offered love,　355
　　　When it comes clad in secrets.

CALIANAX.　⟨*aside.*⟩ If I say I will not, he will kill me, I doe see't
　　　writ in his lookes; and should I say I will, heele run and tell the
　　　King: I doe not shun your friendship deere *Melantius*, but this
　　　cause is weightie, give me but an houre to thinke.　360

MELANTIUS.　Take it, ⟨*aside.*⟩— I know this goes unto the King,
　　　But I am arm'd.

　　　　　　　　　　　　　　　　　Exit MELANTIUS.

CALIANAX.　Me thinkes I feele my selfe
　　　But twenty now agen, this fighting foole
　　　Wants policie, I shall revenge my girle,　365
　　　And make her red againe, I pray, my legges
　　　Will last that pace that I will carrie them,
　　　I shall want breath before I finde the King.

　　　　　　　　　　　　　　　　　　　　⟨*Exit.*⟩

ACT IV

⟨SCENE I⟩

Enter MELANTIUS, EVADNE *and a* LADY.

MELANTIUS.　God save you.

EVADNE.　Save you sweete brother.

MELANTIUS.   In my blunt eye me thinkes you looke *Evadne* —
EVADNE.   Come, you would make me blush.
MELANTIUS.   I would *Evadne*, I shall displease my ends els.   5
EVADNE.   You shall if you commend me, I am bashfull,
    Come sir, how doe I looke?
MELANTIUS.   I would not have your women heare me
    Breake into commendations of you, tis not seemely.
EVADNE.   Goe waite me in the gallerie — now speake.   10

                              Exit LADY.

MELANTIUS.   Ile lock the dore first.
EVADNE.   Why?
MELANTIUS.   I will not have your guilded things that daunce
    In visitation with their millan skins
    Choake up my businesse.   15
EVADNE.   You are strangely dispos'd sir.
MELANTIUS.   Good Madame, not to make you merry.
EVADNE.   No, if you praise me, twill make me sad.
MELANTIUS.   Such a sad commendations I have for you.
EVADNE.   Brother, the Court has made you wittie,   20
    And learne to riddle.
MELANTIUS.   I praise the Court for't, has it learnd you nothing?
EVADNE.   Me?
MELANTIUS.   I *Evadne*, thou art yong and hansome,
    A Lady of a sweete complexion,   25
    And such a flowing carriage, that it cannot
    Chuse but inflame a Kingdome.
EVADNE.   Gentle brother.
MELANTIUS.   Tis yet in thy repentance, foolish woman,
    To make me gentle.   30
EVADNE.   How is this?
MELANTIUS.   Tis base,
    And I could blush at these yeares, through all
    My honord scars; to come to such a parlie.
EVADNE.   I understand ye not.   35

IV. I. 3 *Evadne*—] ~. Qq. *Evadne here checks Melantius' blunt comment, but
asks him to speak on four lines later. Dyce and Daniel print the line as in* Qq.
    11 the dore] Q2; your dores Q1.

MELANTIUS.   You dare not foole,
   They that commit thy faults flie the remembrance.
EVADNE.   My faults sir, I would have you know I care not
   If they were written here, here in my forehead.
MELANTIUS.   Thy body is to little for the story,   40
   The lusts of which would fill another woman,
   Though she had twins within her.
EVADNE.   This is saucie,
   Looke you intrude no more, theres your way.
MELANTIUS.   Thou art my way, and I will tread upon thee,   45
   Till I finde truth out.
EVADNE.   What truth is that you looke for?
MELANTIUS.   Thy long lost honor: would the gods had set me
   Rather to grapple with the plague, or stand
   One of their loudest bolts, come tell me quickly,   50
   Doe it without inforcement, and take heede
   You swell me not above my temper.
EVADNE.   How sir? where got you this report?
MELANTIUS.   Where there was people in every place.
EVADNE.   They and the seconds of it are base people,   55
   Beleeve them not, they lied.
MELANTIUS.   Doe not play with mine anger, doe not wretch,
   I come to know that desperate foole that drew thee
   From thy faire life, be wise and lay him open.
EVADNE.   Unhand me and learne manners, such another   60
   Forgetfulnesse forfits your life.
MELANTIUS.   Quench me this mighty humor, and then tell me
   Whose whore you are, for you are one, I know it,
   Let all mine honors perish but ile finde him,
   Though he lie lockt up in thy blood, be sudden,   65
   There is no facing it, and be not flattered,
   The burnt aire when the dog raines, is not fouler
   Then thy contagious name, till thy repentance
   (If the gods grant thee any) purge thy sicknesse.
EVADNE.   Begon, you are my brother, thats your safty.   70
MELANTIUS.   Ile be a woulfe first, tis to be thy brother
   An infamy below the sin of coward:
   I am as far from being part of thee,
   As thou art from thy vertue, seeke a kindred

Mongst sensuall beasts, and make a goate thy brother,   75
A goate is cooler; will you tell me yet?

EVADNE.   If you stay here and raile thus, I shall tell you,
Ile ha you whipt, get you to your command,
And there preach to your Centinels,
And tell them what a brave man you are, I shal laugh at you.   80

MELANTIUS.   Y'are growne a glorious whore, where bee your
Fighters? what mortall foole durst raise thee to this daring,
And I alive? by my just sword, h'ad safer
Bestride a billow when the angry North
Plowes up the sea, or made heavens fire his foe;   85
Worke me no hier, will you discover yet?

EVADNE.   The fellowes mad, sleepe and speake sence.

MELANTIUS.   Force my swolne heart no further, I would save
    thee,
Your great maintainers are not here, they dare not,
Would they were al, and armed, I would speake loud,   90
Heres one should thunder to 'em: will you tell me?
Thou hast no hope to scape, he that dares most,
And dams away his soule to doe thee service,
Will sooner snatch meat from a hungry Lyon
Then come to rescue thee; thou hast death about thee: 95
Has undone thine honour, poyson'd thy vertue,
And of a lovely rose, left thee a canker.

EVADNE.   Let me consider.

MELANTIUS.   Doe, whose child thou wert,
Whose honor thou hast murdered, whose grave opened,   100
And so pul'd on the gods, that in their justice
They must restore him flesh agen and life,
And raise his drie bones to revenge this scandall.

EVADNE.   The gods are not of my minde, they had better
Let 'em lie sweete still in the earth, theile stinke here.   105

MELANTIUS.   Doe you raise mirth out of my easinesse?
Forsake me then all weaknesses of nature,
That make men women, speake you whore, speake truth,
Or by the deare soule of thy sleeping father
This sword shall be thy lover, tell or ile kill thee,   110
And when thou hast told all, thou wilt deserve it.

76 brother] Q2; father Q1.

EVADNE.   You will not murther me.

MELANTIUS.   No, tis a justice and a noble one,
To put the light out of such base offenders.

EVADNE.   Helpe.   115

MELANTIUS.   By thy foule selfe, no humaine help shall help thee,
If thou criest, when I have kild thee, as I have
Vow'd to doe, if thou confesse not, naked as thou hast left
Thine honor, will I leave thee,
That on thy branded flesh the world may reade   120
Thy blacke shame and my justice, wilt thou bend yet?

EVADNE.   Yes.

MELANTIUS.   Up and beginne your storie.

EVADNE.   Oh I am miserable.

MELANTIUS.   Tis true, thou art, speake truth still.   125

EVADNE.   I have offended, noble Sir, forgive me.

MELANTIUS.   With what secure slave?

EVADNE.   Doe not aske me Sir,
Mine owne remembrance is a miserie
Too mightie for me.   130

MELANTIUS.   Doe not fall backe agen, my sword's unsheathed yet.

EVADNE.   What shall I doe?

MELANTIUS.   Be true, and make your fault lesse.

EVADNE.   I dare not tell.

MELANTIUS.   Tell, or ile be this day a killing thee.   135

EVADNE.   Will you forgive me then?

MELANTIUS.   Stay, I must aske mine honour first, I have too
much foolish nature in me, speake.

EVADNE.   Is there none else here?

MELANTIUS.   None but a fearfull conscience, that's too many.   140
Who ist?

EVADNE.   Oh heare me gently, it was the King.

MELANTIUS.   No more. My worthy fathers and my services
Are liberally rewarded: King I thanke thee,
For all my dangers and my wounds thou hast paid me   145
In my owne metall, these are souldiers thankes.
How long have you lived thus *Evadne*?

EVADNE.   Too long.

MELANTIUS.   Too late you find it, can you be sorry?

EVADNE.   Would I were halfe as blamelesse.   150

MELANTIUS.   *Evadne*, thou wilt to thy trade againe.
EVADNE.   First to my grave.
MELANTIUS.   Would gods thou hadst beene so blest:
   Dost thou not hate this King now? prethee hate him.
   Could'st thou not curse him, I command thee curse him,   155
   Curse till the gods heare and deliver him
   To thy just wishes, yet I feare *Evadne*
   You had rather play your game out.
EVADNE.   No, I feele
   Too many sad confusions here to let in   160
   Any loose flame hereafter.
MELANTIUS.   Dost thou not feele amongst al those one brave anger
   That breakes out nobly, and directs thine arme
   To kill this base King?
EVADNE.   All the gods forbid it.   165
MELANTIUS.   No al the gods require it, they are dishonored in him.
EVADNE.   Tis too fearfull.
MELANTIUS.   Y'are valiant in his bed, and bold enough
   To be a stale whore, and have your Madams name
   Discourse for groomes and pages, and hereafter   170
   When his coole Majestie hath laid you by
   To be at pension with some needie Sir
   For meat and courser cloathes, thus farre you knew no feare,
   Come you shall kill him.
EVADNE.   Good sir.   175
MELANTIUS.   And twere to kisse him dead, thoudst smother him.
   Be wise and kill him: canst thou live and know
   What noble minds shall make thee see thy selfe,
   Found out with every finger, made the shame
   Of all successions, and in this great ruine   180
   Thy brother and thy noble husband broken?
   Thou shalt not live thus, kneele and sweare to helpe me
   When I shall call thee to it, or by all
   Holy in heaven and earth thou shalt not live
   To breathe a full houre longer, not a thought.   185
   Come tis a righteous oath, give me thy hand,
   And both to heaven held up, sweare by that wealth
   This lustfull theefe stole from thee, when I say it,
   To let his foule soule out.

EVADNE.   Here I sweare it,   190
    And all you spirits of abused Ladies
    Helpe me in this performance.
MELANTIUS.   Enough, this must be knowne to none
    But you and I *Evadne*, not to your Lord,
    Though he be wise and noble, and a fellow   195
    Dare step as farre into a worthy action,
    As the most daring, I as farre as justice.
    Aske me not why. Farewell.

Exit MELANTIUS.

EVADNE.   Would I could say so to my blacke disgrace,
    Gods where have I beene all this time; how friended,   200
    That I should lose my selfe thus desperately,
    And none for pittie shew me how I wandred?
    There is not in the compasse of the light
    A more unhappy creature, sure I am monstrous,
    For I have done those follies, those mad mischiefes   205
    Would dare a woman. O my loaden soule,
    Be not so cruell to me, choake not up
    The way to my repentance.

Enter AMINTOR.

    O my Lord.
AMINTOR.   How now?   210
EVADNE.   My much abused Lord.   *Kneele.*
AMINTOR.   This cannot be.
EVADNE.   I doe not kneele to live, I dare not hope it,
    The wrongs I did are greater, looke upon me
    Though I appeare with all my faults.   215
AMINTOR.   Stand up.
    This is a new way to beget more sorrowes,
    Heaven knowes I have too many, doe not mocke me,
    Though I am tame and bred up with my wrongs,
    Which are my foster-brothers, I may leape   220
    Like a hand-wolfe into my naturall wildnesse,
    And doe an outrage, prethee doe not mocke me.
EVADNE.   My whole life is so leaprous it infects
    All my repentance, I would buy your pardon

Though at the highest set, even with my life,   225
That sleight contrition, that; no sacrifice
For what I have committed.
AMINTOR.   Sure I dazle.
There cannot be a faith in that foule woman
That knowes no God more mighty then her mischiefes,   230
Thou doest still worse, still number on thy faults,
To presse my poore heart thus. Can I beleeve
Theres any seed of vertue in that woman
Left to shoot up, that dares goe on in sinne
Knowne and so knowne as thine is? O *Evadne*,   235
Would there were any safetie in thy sex,
That I might put a thousand sorrowes off,
And credit thy repentance, but I must not,
Thou hast brought me to that dull calamitie,
To that strange misbeleefe of all the world,   240
And all things that are in it, that I feare
I shall fall like a tree, and finde my grave,
Only remembring that I grieve.
EVADNE.   My Lord,
Give me your griefes, you are an innocent,   245
A soule as white as heaven, let not my sinnes
Perish your noble youth, I doe not fall here
To shadow by dissembling with my teares,
As all say women can, or to make lesse
What my hot will hath done, which heaven and you   250
Knowes to be tougher then the hand of time
Can cut from mans remembrance, no I doe not,
I doe appeare the same, the same *Evadne*,
Drest in the shames I liv'd in, the same monster.
But these are names of honour to what I am,   255
I doe present my selfe the foulest creature,
Most poisonous, dangerous, and despisde of men
Lerna ere bred or *Nilus*, I am hell,
Till you my deare Lord shoot your light into me,
The beames of your forgivenesse, I am soule sicke,   260
And wither with the feare of one condemnd
Till I have got your pardon.
AMINTOR.   Rise *Evadne*.

Those heavenly powers that put this good into thee
Grant a continuance of it, I forgive thee,   265
Make thy selfe worthy of it, and take heed,
Take heed *Evadne* this be serious,
Mocke not the powers above, that can, and dare
Give thee a great example of their justice
To all insuing eies, if thou plai'st   270
With thy repentance, the best sacrifice.

EVADNE.   I have done nothing good to win beleife,
My life hath beene so faithlesse, all the Creatures
Made for heavens honors have their ends, and good ones,
Al but the cousening *Crocodiles*, false women.   275
They raigne here like those plagues, those killing soares
Men pray against, and when they die, like tales
Ill told, and unbeleiv'd they passe away,
And go to dust forgotten: But my Lord
Those short daies I shall number to my rest,   280
(As many must not see me,) shall though too late,
Though in my evening, yet perceive a will
Since I can doe no good because a woman,
Reach constantly at something that is neere it,
I will redeeme one minute of my age,   285
Or like another *Niobe* ile weepe
Till I am water.

AMINTOR.   I am now dissolved.
My frozen soule melts: may each sin thou hast,
Finde a new mercy: rise, I am at peace: 290
Hadst thou beene thus, thus excellently good,
Before that devill King tempted thy frailty,
Sure thou hadst made a Star, give me thy hand,
From this time I will know thee, and as far
As honour gives me leave, be thy *Amintor*,   295
When we meete next I will salute thee fairely,
And pray the gods to give thee happy daies,
My Charity shall go along with thee,
Though my embraces must be far from thee,
I should ha' kild thee, but this sweete repentance   300
Lockes up my vengeance, for which, thus I kisse thee,
The last kisse we must take, and would to heaven

The holy Preist that gave our hands together,
Had given us equall virtues, go *Evadne*,
The gods thus part our bodies, have a care 305
My honour falles no further, I am well then.
EVADNE. All the deare joyes here, and above hereafter
Crowne thy faire soul, thus I take leave my Lord,
And never shall you see the foule *Evadne*
Till she have tried all honoured meanes that may 310
Set her in rest, and wash her staines away.

Exeunt.

⟨ACT IV⟩

⟨SCENE II⟩

Hoboies play within.
Banquet. Enter KING, CALIANAX.

KING. I cannot tell how I should credit this
From you that are his enemie.
CALIANAX. I am sure he said it to me, and ile justifie it
What way he dares oppose, but with my sword.
KING. But did he breake without all circumstance 5
To you his Foe, that he would have the fort
To kill me, and then scape?
CALIANAX. If he deny it, ile make him blush.
KING. It sounds incredibly.
CALIANAX. I so does every thing I say of late. 10
KING. Not so *Callianax*.
CALIANAX. Yes I should sit
Mute whilst a Rogue with strong armes cuts your throate.
KING. Well I will trie him, and if this be true
Ile pawne my life ile finde it, ift be false 15
And that you cloath your hate in such a lie,
You shall hereafter doate in your owne house,
Not in the Court.
CALIANAX. Why if it be a lie
Mine eares are false, for Ile be sworne I heard it: 20

Old men are good for nothing, you were best
Put me to death for hearing, and free him
For meaning it, you would a trusted me
Once, but the time is altered.

KING. And will still where I may doe with justice to the world, 25
you have no witnesse.

CALIANAX. Yes my selfe.

KING. No more I meane there were that heard it.

CALIANAX. How no more? would you have more? why am not I
enough to hang a thousand Rogues? 30

KING. But so you may hang honest men too if you please.

CALIANAX. I may, tis like I will doe so, there are a hundred will
sweare it for a need too, if I say it.

KING. Such witnesses we need not.

CALIANAX. And tis hard if my word cannot hang a boisterous 35
knave.

KING. Enough, where's *Strato*?

Enter STRATO.

STRATO. Sir.

KING. Why wheres all the Company? call *Amintor* in,
Evadne, wheres my brother, and *Melantius*? 40
Bid him come too, and *Diphilus*, call all
That are without there:

Exit STRATO.

If he should desire
The combat of you, tis not in the power
Of all our lawes to hinder it, unlesse 45
We meane to quit 'em.

CALIANAX. Why if you doe thinke
Tis fit an old man, and a Counsellor
To fight for what he saies, then you may grant it.

Enter AMINTOR, EVADNE, MELANTIUS, DIPHILUS,
LISIPPUS, CLEON, STRATO, DIAGORAS.

KING.   Come sirs, *Amintor* thou art yet a Bridegroome,   50
    And I will use thee so, thou shalt sit downe,
    Evadne sit, and you *Amintor* too,
    This banquet is for you sir: who has brought
    A merry tale about him, to raise laughter
    Amongst our wine? why *Strato* where art thou?   55
    Thou wilt chop out with them unseasonably
    When I desire 'em not.
STRATO.   Tis my ill lucke Sir, so to spend them then.
KING.   Reach me a boule of wine: *Melantius* thou art sad.
AMINTOR.   I should be Sir the merriest here,   60
    But I ha nere a story of mine owne
    Worth telling at this time.
KING.   Give me the wine.
    Melantius I am now considering
    How easie twere for any man we trust   65
    To poyson one of us in such a boule.
MELANTIUS.   I thinke it were not hard Sir, for a Knave.
CALIANAX.   Such as you are.
KING.   Ifaith twere easie, it becomes us well
    To get plaine dealing men about our selves,   70
    Such as you all are here, *Amintor* to thee
    And to thy faire *Evadne*.
MELANTIUS.   [*aside*.] Have you thought of this *Callianax*?
CALIANAX.   Yes marry have I.
MELANTIUS.   And whats your resolution?   75
CALIANAX.   Ye shall have it soundly I warrant you.
KING.   Reach to *Amintor*, *Strato*.
AMINTOR.   Here my love,
    This wine will doe thee wrong, for it will set
    Blushes upon thy cheekes, and till thou dost   80
    A fault twere pitty.
KING.   Yet I wonder much
    Of the strange desperation of these men,
    That dare attempt such acts here in our state,

IV. II. 59 AMINTOR] Q2; MEL Q1.

He could not scape that did it.   85
MELANTIUS.   Were he knowne, unpossible.
KING.   It would be knowne *Melantius*.
MELANTIUS.   It ought to be, if he got then away
  He must weare all our lives upon his sword,
  He need not flie the Iland, he must leave   90
  No one alive.
KING.   No, I should thinke no man
  Could kill me and scape cleare, but that old man.
CALIANAX.   But I? heaven blesse me, I, should I my liege?
KING.   I do not thinke thou wouldst, but yet thou mightst,   95
  For thou hast in thy hands the meanes to scape,
  By keeping of the fort, he has *Melantius*,
  And he has kept it well.
MELANTIUS.   From Cobwebs Sir,
  Tis cleane swept, I can finde no other Art   100
  In keeping of it now, twas nere besieg'd
  Since he commaunded.
CALIANAX.   I shall be sure of your good word,
  But I have kept it safe from such as you.
MELANTIUS.   Keepe your ill temper in,   105
  I speake no malice, had my brother kept it
  I should ha sed as much.
KING.   You are not merry, brother drinke wine,
  Sit you all still, [*aside.*] *Callianax*
  I cannot trust thus, I have throwne out words   110
  That would have fetcht warme bloud upon the cheekes
  Of guilty men, and he is never mov'd,
  He knowes no such thing.
CALIANAX.   Impudence may scape, when feeble virtue is accus'd.
KING.   A must if he were guilty feele an alteration   115
  At this our whisper, whilst we point at him,
  You see he does not.
CALIANAX.   Let him hang himselfe,
  What care I what he does, this he did say.
KING.   *Melantius* you can easily conceive   120
  What I have meant, for men that are in fault
  Can subtly apprehend when others aime
  At what they doe amisse, but I forgive

    Freely before this man, heaven doe so too;
    I will not touch thee so much as with shame   125
    Of telling it, let it be so no more.
CALIANAX.   Why this is very fine.
MELANTIUS.   I cannot tell
    What tis you meane, but I am apt enough
    Rudely to thrust into ignorant fault,   130
    But let me know it, happily tis naught
    But misconstruction, and where I am cleare
    I will not take forgivenesse of the gods,
    Much lesse of you.
KING.   Nay if you stand so stiffe, I shall call back my mercy.   135
MELANTIUS.   I want smoothnes
    To thanke a man for pardoning of a crime
    I never knew.
KING.   Not to instruct your knowledge, but to show you my
    eares are every where, you meant to kill me, and get the fort to 140
    scape.
MELANTIUS.   Pardon me Sir,
    My bluntnesse will be pardoned, you preserve
    A race of idle people here about you,
    Eaters, and talkers, to defame the worth   145
    Of those that doe things worthy, the man that uttered this
    Had perisht without food, bee't who it will,
    But for this arme that fenst him from the Foe.
    And if I thought you gave a faith to this,
    The plainenesse of my nature would speake more,   150
    Give me a pardon (for you ought to doo't)
    To kill him that spake this.
CALIANAX.   ⟨aside.⟩ I that will be the end of all,
    Then I am fairely paide for all my care and service.
MELANTIUS.   That old man, who calls me enemy, and of whom I 155
    (Though I will never match my hate so low,)
    Have no good thought, would yet I thinke excuse me,
    And sweare he thought me wrong'd in this.

---

145 Eaters] Q2; Facers Q1. *Most edd. except* Q1's *more striking reading. But* Q2 *is clearly a correction of* Q1, *and* Q1 *is easily derived from a simple pair of ms. misreadings.* Eaters *in conjunction with* talkers *is the more pointed term to use at a banquet.* Melantius *elaborates his usage in* without food *two lines later.*

CALIANAX.   Who I, thou shamelesse Fellow, didst thou not
  speake to me of it thy self?   160
MELANTIUS.   O then it came from him.
CALIANAX.   From me, who should it come from but from me?
MELANTIUS.   Nay I beleeve your malice is enough,
  But I ha lost my anger, Sir I hope
  You are well satisfied.   165
KING.   *Lisippus*: cheare *Amintor* and his Lady, theres no sound
  Comes from you, I will come and doo't my selfe.
AMINTOR.   You have done already Sir for me I thanke you.
KING.   *Melantius* I doe credit this from him,
  How sleight so ere you mak't.   170
MELANTIUS.   Tis strange you should.
CALIANAX.   Tis strange a should beleeve an old mans word,
  That never lied ins life.
MELANTIUS.   I talke not to thee,
  Shall the wilde words of this distempered man,   175
  Frantique with age and sorrow, make a breach
  Betwixt your Majestie and me? twas wrong
  To harken to him, but to credit him
  As much, at least, as I have power to beare.
  But pardon me, whilst I speake onely truth,   180
  I may commend my selfe — I have bestowd
  My carelesse bloud with you, and should be loath
  To thinke an action that would make me loose
  That, and my thankes too: when I was a boy
  I thrust my selfe into my Countries cause,   185
  And did a deed, that pluckt five yeares from time
  And stil'd me man then, and for you my king
  Your Subjects all have fed by vertue of my arme,
  This sword of mine hath plowd the ground,
  And reapt the fruit in peace;   190
  And you your selfe have liv'd at home in ease:
  So terrible I grew that without swords
  My name hath fetcht you conquest, and my heart
  And limmes are still the same, my will as great
  To doe you service: let me not be paid   195
  With such a strange distrust.
KING.   *Melantius* I held it great injustice to beleeve

Thine enemie, and did not, if I did,
I doe not, let that satisfie: what strooke
With sadnesse all? more wine.   200

CALIANAX.   A few fine words have overthrowne my truth,
A th'art a Villaine.

MELANTIUS.   [*aside.*] Why thou wert better let me have the fort,
Dotard, I will disgrace thee thus for ever,
There shall no credit lie upon thy words,   205
Thinke better and deliver it.

CALIANAX.   My leige, hees at me now agen to doe it, speake,
Denie it if thou canst, examine him
Whilst he is hot, for if hee coole agen,
He will forsweare it.   210

KING.   This is lunacie I hope, *Melantius.*

MELANTIUS.   He hath lost himselfe
Much since his daughter mist the happinesse
My sister gaind, and though he call me Foe,
I pittie him.   215

CALIANAX.   A pittie a pox upon you.

MELANTIUS.   Marke his disordered words, and at the Maske
Diagoras knowes he rag'd, and raild at me,
And cald a Ladie Whore so innocent
She understood him not, but it becomes   220
Both you and me to forgive distraction,
Pardon him as I doe.

CALIANAX.   Ile not speake for thee, for all thy cunning, if you
will be safe chop off his head, for there was never knowne so
impudent a Rascall.   225

KING.   Some that love him get him to bed: why, pittie should not
let age make it selfe contemptible, we must be all old, have him
away.

MELANTIUS.   *Callianax* the King beleeves you, come, you shall
go home, and rest, you ha done well, ⟨*aside*⟩ youle give it up   230
when I have usd you thus a month, I hope.

CALIANAX.   Now, now, tis plaine Sir, he does move me still,
He saies he knowes ile give him up the fort
When he has usd me thus a month, I am mad
Am I not still?   235

OMNES.   Ha ha ha.

CALIANAX.   I shall be mad indeed if you doe thus,
  Why should you trust a sturdie fellow there,
  (That has no virtue in him, alls in his sword)
  Before me? doe but take his weapons from him   240
  And hees an Asse, and I am a very foole
  Both with him, and without him, as you use me.
OMNES.   Ha ha ha.
KING.   Tis well, *Calianax*: but if you use
  This once agen I shall intreat some other   245
  To see your offices be well dischargd.
  Be merry Gentlemen, it growes somewhat late,
  Amintor thou wouldst be a bed agen.
AMINTOR.   Yes Sir.
KING.   And you *Evadne*.   250
  Let me take thee in my armes, *Melantius*, and beleeve
  Thou art as thou deservest to be, my freind,
  Still, and for ever. Good *Callianax*
  Sleepe soundly, it will bring thee to thy selfe.

    Exeunt OMNES. *Manent* MELANTIUS *and* CALIANAX.

CALIANAX.   Sleepe soundly! I sleepe soundly now I hope,   255
  I could not be thus else. How dar'st thou stay
  Alone with me, knowing how thou hast used me?
MELANTIUS.   You cannot blast me with your tongue,
  And thats the strongest part you have about you.
CALIANAX.   I doe looke for some great punishment for this,   260
  For I beginne to forget all my hate,
  And tak't unkindly that mine enemy
  Should use me so extremely scurvily.
MELANTIUS.   I shall melt too, if you begin to take
  Unkindnesses; I never meant you hurt.   265
CALIANAX.   Thoult anger me agen; thou wretched roague,
  Meant me no hurt! disgrace me with the King,
  Lose all my offices, this is no hurt
  Is it? I prethee what dost thou call hurt?
MELANTIUS.   To poison men because they love me not,   270
  To call the credit of mens wives in question,
  To murder children, betwixt me and Land;
  This I call hurt.

CALIANAX.   All this thou thinkst is sport,
  For mine is worse, but use thy will with me   275
  For betwixt griefe and anger I could crie.
MELANTIUS.   Be wise then and be safe, thou maist revenge.
CALIANAX.   I oth'King, I would revenge of thee.
MELANTIUS.   That you must plot your selfe.
CALIANAX.   I am a fine plotter.   280
MELANTIUS.   The short is, I will hold thee with the King
  In this perplexitie till peevishnesse
  And his disgrace have laid thee in thy grave:
  But if thou wilt deliver up the fort,
  Ile take thy trembling body in my armes,   285
  And beare thee over dangers, thou shalt hold
  Thy wonted state.
CALIANAX.   If I should tell the King, canst thou deni't agen?
MELANTIUS.   Trie and beleeve.
CALIANAX.   Nay then thou canst bring any thing about,   290
  Melantius, thou shalt have the fort.
MELANTIUS.   Why well, here let our hate be buried, and
  This hand shall right us both, give me thy aged brest
  To compasse.
CALIANAX.   Nay I doe not love thee yet,   295
  I cannot well endure to looke on thee,
  And if I thought it were a curtesie,
  Thou shouldst not have it, but I am disgrac't,
  My offices are to be tane away,
  And if I did but hold this fort a day,   300
  I doe beleeve the King would take it from me,
  And give it thee, things are so strangely carried:
  Nere thanke me for't, but yet the King shall know
  There was some such thing int I told him of,
  And that I was an honest man.   305
MELANTIUS.   Heele buy that knowledge very deerely:

Enter DIPHILUS.

Diphilus, what newes with thee?

283 his] Q1; thy Q2. Q2 *normalises, but* Q1 (*the King's disgracing of Calianax*)
makes good sense.

DIPHILUS.   This were a night indeed to doe it in,
    The King hath sent for her.
MELANTIUS.   She shall performe it then, goe *Diphilus*   310
    And take from this good man my worthy friend
    The fort, heele give it thee.
DIPHILUS.   Ha you got that?
CALIANAX.   Art thou of the same breed? canst thou denie
    This to the King too?   315
DIPHILUS.   With a confidence as great as his.
CALIANAX.   Faith like enough.
MELANTIUS.   Away and use him kindly.
CALIANAX.   Touch not me, I hate the whole straine, if thou
    follow me a great way off, Ile give thee up the fort, and hang   320
    your selves.
MELANTIUS.   Be gone.
DIPHILUS.   Hees finely wrought.

                           Exeunt CALIANAX, DIPHILUS.

MELANTIUS.   This is a night spight of Astronomers
    To doe the deed in, I will wash the staine   325
    That rests upon our house, off with his bloud.

Enter AMINTOR.

AMINTOR.   *Melantius* now assist me if thou beest
    That which thou saist, assist me, I have lost
    All my distempers, and have found a rage
    So pleasing, helpe me.   330
MELANTIUS.   Who can see him thus,
    And not sweare vengeance? whats the matter friend?
AMINTOR.   Out with thy sword, and hand in hand with me
    Rush to the chamber of this hated King,
    And sinke him with the weight of all his sins   335
    To hell for ever.
MELANTIUS.   Twere a rash attempt,
    Not to be done with safetie, let your reason
    Plot your revenge, and not your passion.
AMINTOR.   If thou refusest me in these extremes,   340
    Thou art no friend: he sent for her to me,
    By heaven to me, my selfe, and I must tell ye
    I love her as a stranger, there is worth

In that vild woman, worthy things *Melantius*,
And she repents, Ile doo't my selfe alone,   345
Though I be slaine, farewell.
MELANTIUS.   ⟨*aside.*⟩ Heele overthrow my whole designe with
    madnes,
Amintor, thinke what thou doest, I dare as much as valour,
But tis the King, the King, the King, *Amintor*,
With whom thou fightest. [*aside.*] I know hees honest,   350
And this will worke with him.
AMINTOR.   I cannot tell
What thou hast said, but thou hast charmd my sword
Out of my hand, and left me shaking here
Defencelesse.   355
MELANTIUS.   I will take it up for thee.
AMINTOR.   What a wilde beast is uncollected man!
The thing that we call honour beares us all
Headlong into sinne, and yet it selfe is nothing.
MELANTIUS.   Alas how variable are thy thoughts?   360
AMINTOR.   Just like my fortunes, I was run to that
I purposd to have chid thee for. Some plot
I did distrust thou hadst against the King
By that old fellowes carriage, but take heed,
Theres not the least limbe growing to a King   365
But carries thunder in't.
MELANTIUS.   I have none against him.
AMINTOR.   Why come then, and still remember wee may not
    thinke revenge.
MELANTIUS.   I will remember.

                                    Exeunt.

ACT V

⟨SCENE I⟩

Enter EVADNE *and a* GENTLEMAN.

EVADNE.   Sir is the King abed?
GENTLEMAN.   Madam an houre agoe.
EVADNE.   Give me the key then, and let none be neere.
Tis the Kings pleasure.

GENTLEMAN.   I understand you Madam, would twere mine,   5
    I must not wish good rest unto your Ladiship.
EVADNE.   You talke, you talke.
GENTLEMAN.   Tis all I dare doe Madam, but the King will wake,
     and then me thinkes —
EVADNE.   Saving your imagination, pray, good night Sir.   10
GENTLEMAN.   A good night be it then, and a long one Madam, I
    am gone.

                                              Exit.

KING *a bed.*

EVADNE.   The night growes horrible, and all about me
    Like my blacke purpose, O the conscience
    Of a lost virgin, whither wilt thou pull me?   15
    To what things dismall, as the depth of hell,
    Wilt thou provoke me? Let no woman dare
    From this houre be disloyall, if her heart
    Be flesh, if she have bloud and can feare, tis a madnesse
    Above that desperate fooles that left his peace,   20
    And went to sea to fight, tis so many sins,
    An age cannot repent 'em, and so great,
    The gods want mercy for, yet I must through 'em
    I have begun a slaughter on my honour,
    And I must end it there; a sleepes, oh God,   25
    Why give you peace to this untemperate beast,
    That hath so long transgrest you? I must kill him,
    And I will doo't bravely: the meere joy
    Tels me I merit in it, yet I must not
    Thus tamely doe it as he sleepes, that were   30
    To rock him to another world, my vengeance
    Shall seaze him waking, and then lay before him
    The number of his wrongs and punishments.
    Ile shape his sins like furies till I waken
    His evill Angell, his sicke conscience,   35
    And then Ile strike him dead. King by your leave,

                           Ties his armes to the bed.

I dare not trust your strength, your Grace and I

Must grapple upon even tearmes no more.
So, if he raile me not from my resolution,
I shall be strong enough.   40
My Lord the King, my Lord, a sleepes
As if he meant to wake no more, my Lord,
Is he not dead already? Sir, my Lord.
KING.   Whose that?
EVADNE.   O you sleepe soundly Sir.   45
KING.   My deare *Evadne*,
I have beene dreaming of thee, come to bed.
EVADNE.   I am come at length Sir, but how welcome?
KING.   What prettie new device is this *Evadne?*
What, doe you tie me to you by my love?   50
This is a queint one: come my deare and kisse me,
Ile be thy *Mars*, to bed my Queene of love,
Let us be caught together, that the gods may see,
And envie our embraces.
EVADNE.   Stay Sir, stay,   55
You are too hot, and I have brought you physicke,
To temper your high veines.
KING.   Prethee to bed then, let me take it warme,
Here thou shalt know the state of my body better.
EVADNE.   I know you have a surfeited foule body,   60
And you must bleed.
KING.   Bleed!
EVADNE.   I you shall bleed, lie still, and if the devill
Your lust will give you leave, repent, this steele
Comes to redeeme the honour that you stole   65
King, my faire name, which nothing but thy death
Can answer to the world.
KING.   How's this *Evadne?*
EVADNE.   I am not she, nor beare I in this breast
So much cold spirit to be cald a woman,   70
I am a Tiger, I am any thing
That knowes not pittie, stirre not, if thou doest,
Ile take thee unprepar'd, thy feares upon thee,
That make thy sins looke double, and so send thee
(By my revenge I will) to looke those torments   75
Prepar'd for such blacke soules.

KING.   Thou doest not meane this, tis impossible,
  Thou art too sweet and gentle.
EVADNE.   No I am not,
  I am as foule as thou art, and can number   80
  As many such hels here: I was once faire,
  Once I was lovely, not a blowing rose
  More chastly sweet, till thou, thou, thou foule canker,
  (Stirre not) didst poison me, I was a world of vertue
  Till your curst Court and you (hell blesse you for't)   85
  With your temptations on temptations
  Made me give up mine honour, for which (King)
  I am come to kill thee.
KING.   No.
EVADNE.   I am.   90
KING.   Thou art not.
  I prethee speake not these things, thou art gentle,
  And wert not meant thus rugged.
EVADNE.   Peace and heare me.
  Stirre nothing but your tongue, and that for mercy,   95
  To those above us, by whose lights I vow,
  Those blessed fires, that shot to see our sinne,
  If thy hot soule had substance with thy bloud,
  I would kill that too, which being past my steele,
  My tongue shall reach: Thou art a shamelesse villaine,   100
  A thing out of the overcharge of nature,
  Sent like a thicke cloud to disperse a plague
  Upon weake catching women, such a tyrant,
  That for his lust would sell away his subjects,
  I all his heaven hereafter.   105
KING.   Heare *Evadne*,
  Thou soule of sweetnesse, heare, I am thy King.
EVADNE.   Thou art my shame, lie still, theres none about you
  Within your cries, all promises of safetie
  Are but deluding dreames, thus, thus thou foule man,   110
  Thus I begin my vengeance.

Stabs him.

v. I. 111 S.D *Stabs him.*] Q2; *om.* Q1. Q1 *gives a similar direction later, at line* 118.

KING.   Hold *Evadne*,
  I doe command thee, hold.
EVADNE.   I doe not meane Sir
  To part so fairely with you, we must change   115
  More of these love-trickes yet.
KING.   What bloudie villaine
  Provok't thee to this murther?
EVADNE.   Thou, thou monster.
KING.   Oh.   120
EVADNE.   Thou kepst me brave at Court, and whorde me, King,
  Then married me to a young noble Gentleman,
  And whorde me still.
KING.   *Evadne*, pittie me.
EVADNE.   Hell take me then, this for my Lord *Amintor*,   125
  This for my noble brother, and this stroke
  For the most wrong'd of women.

Kils him.

KING.   Oh I die.
EVADNE.   Die all our faults together, I forgive thee.

Exit.

Enter two ⟨LORDS.⟩ *of the Bed-chamber.*

FIRST ⟨LORD⟩.   Come now shees gone, lets enter, the King 130
  expects it, and will be angry.
SECOND ⟨LORD⟩.   Tis a fine wench, weele have a snap at her
  one of these nights as she goes from him.
FIRST ⟨LORD⟩.   Content: how quickly he had done with her,
  I see Kings can doe no more that way then other mortall people. 135
SECOND ⟨LORD⟩.   How fast he is! I cannot heare him breathe.
FIRST ⟨LORD⟩.   Either the tapers give a feeble light, or he
  lookes very pale.
SECOND ⟨LORD⟩.   And so he does, pray heaven he be well.
  Lets looke: Alas, hees stiffe, wounded and dead. Treason, treason. 140
FIRST ⟨LORD⟩.   Run forth and call.
SECOND ⟨LORD⟩.   Treason, treason.

Exit SECOND LORD.

FIRST ⟨LORD⟩.   This will be laid on us: who can beleeve
  A woman could doe this?

Enter CLEON *and* LISIPPUS.

CLEON.   How now? wheres the traitor?   145
FIRST ⟨LORD⟩.   Fled, fled away, but there her wofull act
    Lies still.
CLEON.   Her act! a woman!
LISIPPUS.   Wheres the body?
FIRST ⟨LORD⟩.   There.   150
LISIPPUS.   Farewell thou worthy man, there were two bonds
    That tied our loves, a brother and a King,
    The least of which might fetch a floud of teares:
    But such the miserie of greatnesse is,
    They have not time to mourne, then pardon me.   155

Enter STRATO.

    Sirs, which way went she?
STRATO.   Never follow her,
    For she alas was but the instrument.
    Newes is now brought in that *Melantius*
    Has got the Fort, and stands upon the wall,   160
    And with a loud voice cals those few that passe
    At this dead time of night, delivering
    The innocence of this act.
LISIPPUS.   Gentlemen, I am your King.
STRATO.   We doe acknowledge it.   165
LISIPPUS.   I would I were not: follow all, for this must have a
    sudden stop.
                                                        Exeunt.

⟨ACT V⟩

⟨SCENE II⟩

Enter MELANTIUS, DIPHILUS, CALIANAX *on the walls.*

MELANTIUS.   If the dull people can beleeve, I am arm'd.
    Be constant *Diphilus*, now we have time,

    v. ii. i beleeve, I am arm'd.] beleeue I am arm'd, Q1; beleeue I am arm'd. Q2.
The Q1 *compositor misread a full conditional sentence as the first half of one.* Q2
corrects incompletely.

Either to bring our banisht honours home,
Or to create new ones in our ends.

DIPHILUS.   I feare not,   5
  My spirit lies not that way. Courage *Callianax*.

CALIANAX.   Would I had any, you should quickly know it.

MELANTIUS.   Speake to the people, thou art eloquent.

CALIANAX.   Tis a fine eloquence to come to the gallowes,
  You were borne to be my end, the devill take you,   10
  Now must I hang for company, tis strange
  I should be old, and neither wise nor valiant.

Enter LISIPPUS, DIAGORAS, CLEON, STRATO, GUARD.

LISIPPUS.   See where he stands as boldly confident,
  As if he had his full command about him.

STRATO.   He lookes as if he had the better cause, Sir,   15
  Under your gracious pardon let me speake it,
  Though he be mightie spirited and forward
  To all great things, to all things of that danger
  Worse men shake at the telling of, yet certainly
  I doe beleeve him noble, and this action   20
  Rather puld on then sought, his mind was ever
  As worthy as his hand.

LISIPPUS.   Tis my feare too,
  Heaven forgive all: summon him Lord *Cleon*.

CLEON.   Ho from the walls there.   25

MELANTIUS.   Worthy *Cleon* welcome,
  We could a wisht you here Lord, you are honest.

CALIANAX.   [*aside.*] Well thou art as flattering a knave, though
    I dare not tell thee so.

LISIPPUS.   *Melantius.*   30

MELANTIUS.   Sir.

LISIPPUS.   I am sorrie that we meet thus, our old love
  Never requir'd such distance, pray to heaven
  You have not left your selfe, and sought this safetie
  More out of feare then honour, you have lost   35
  A noble master, which your faith, *Melantius*,
  Some thinke might have preserved, yet you know best.

CALIANAX.   ⟨*aside.*⟩ When time was I was mad, some that dares
    fight, I hope will pay this rascall.

MELANTIUS.   Royall young man, those teares looke lovely on   40
    thee,
  Had they beene shed for a deserving one,
  They had beene lasting monuments. Thy brother,
  Whilst he was good, I cald him King, and serv'd him,
  With that strong faith, that most unwearied valour,
  Puld people from the farthest sunne to seeke him,   45
  And buy his friendship. I was then his souldier,
  But since his hot pride drew him to disgrace me,
  And brand my noble actions with his lust,
  (That never-cur'd dishonour of my sister,
  Base staine of whore, and which is worse,   50
  The joy to make it still so) like my selfe,
  Thus I have flung him off with my allegeance,
  And stand here mine owne justice to revenge
  What I have suffred in him, and this old man
  Wrongd almost to lunacie.   55
CALIANAX.   Who I? you wud draw me in: I have had no wrong:
    I doe disclaime ye all.
MELANTIUS.   The short is this;
  Tis no ambition to lift up my selfe
  Urgeth me thus, I doe desire againe   60
  To be a subject, so I may be free;
  If not, I know my strength, and will unbuild
  This goodly towne, be speedie, and be wise, in a replie.
STRATO.   Be sudden Sir to tie
  All up againe, what's done is past recall,   65
  And past you to revenge, and there are thousands
  That wait for such a troubled houre as this.
  Throw him the blanke.
LISIPPUS.   *Melantius*, write in that thy choice,
  My seale is at it.   70
MELANTIUS.   It was our honours drew us to this act,
  No gaine, and we will only worke our pardons.
CALIANAX.   Put my name in too.
DIPHILUS.   You disclaim'd us all but now *Callianax*.
CALIANAX.   Thats all one,   75
  Ile not be hanged hereafter by a tricke,
  Ile have it in.

MELANTIUS.   You shall, you shall:
 Come to the backe gate, and weele call you King,
 And give you up the Fort.   80
LISIPPUS.   Away, away.

           Exeunt OMNES.

      ⟨ACT V⟩

      ⟨SCENE III⟩

   Enter ASPATIA *in mans apparell.*

ASPATIA.   This is my fatall houre, heaven may forgive
 My rash attempt, that causelesly hath laid
 Griefes on me that will never let me rest,
 And put a womans heart into my breast,
 It is more honour for you that I die,   5
 For she that can endure the miserie
 That I have on me, and be patient too,
 May live and laugh at all that you can doe.

Enter SERVANT.

 God save you Sir.
SERVANT.   And you Sir, whats your businesse?   10
ASPATIA.   With you Sir now, to doe me the faire office
 To helpe me to your Lord.
SERVANT.   What would you serve him?
ASPATIA.   Ile doe him any service, but to haste,
 For my affaires are earnest, I desire   15
 To speake with him.
SERVANT.   Sir because you are in such haste, I would be loth to
 delay you longer: you cannot.
ASPATIA.   It shall become you though to tell your Lord.
SERVANT.   Sir he will speake with no body.   20
ASPATIA.   This is most strange: art thou gold proofe? theres for
 thee, helpe me to him.
SERVANT.   Pray be not angry Sir, Ile doe my best.

            Exit.

ASPATIA.   How stubbornly this fellow answer'd me;
  There is a vild dishonest tricke in man,   25
  More then in women: all the men I meet
  Appeare thus to me, are harsh and rude,
  And have a subtletie in every thing,
  Which love could never know; but we fond women
  Harbour the easiest and the smoothest thoughts,   30
  And thinke all shall goe so, it is unjust
  That men and women should be matcht together.

Enter AMINTOR *and his* MAN.

AMINTOR.   Where is he?
SERVANT.   There my Lord.
AMINTOR.   What would you Sir?   35
ASPATIA.   Please it your Lordship to command your man
  Out of the roome, I shall deliver things
  Worthy your hearing.
AMINTOR.   Leave us.

                            ⟨*Exit* SERVANT.⟩

ASPATIA.   [*aside.*] O that that shape should burie falshood in it.   40
AMINTOR.   Now your will Sir.
ASPATIA.   When you know me, my Lord, you needs must ghesse
  My businesse, and I am not hard to know,
  For till the chance of warre markt this smooth face
  With these few blemishes, people would call me   45
  My sisters picture, and her mine: in short,
  I am the brother to the wrong'd *Aspatia.*
AMINTOR.   The wrong'd *Aspatia*, would thou wert so too
  Unto the wrong'd *Amintor*, let me kisse
  That hand of thine in honour that I beare   50
  Unto the wrong'd *Aspatia*, here I stand
  That did it, would I could not: gentle youth
  Leave me, for there is something in thy lookes
  That cals my sins in a most hideous forme
  Into my minde, and I have griefe enough   55
  Without thy helpe.
ASPATIA.   I would I could with credit.

Since I was twelve yeeres old I had not seene
My sister till this houre I now arriv'd;
She sent for me to see her marriage,   60
A wofull one, but they that are above
Have ends in every thing. She usd few words,
But yet enough to make me understand
The basenesse of the injuries you did her.
That little trayning I have had, is war,   65
I may behave my selfe rudely in peace,
I would not though. I shall not need to tell you
I am but young, and would be loth to loose
Honour that is not easily gaind againe;
Fairely I meane to deale. The age is strict   70
For single combats, and we shall be stopt
If it be publisht: if you like your sword
Use it, if mine appeare a better to you,
Change, for the ground is this, and this the time
To end our difference.   75
AMINTOR.   Charitable youth,
 If thou beest such, thinke not I will maintaine
 So strange a wrong, and for thy sisters sake,
 Know, that I could not thinke that desperate thing
 I durst not doe, yet to injoy this world   80
 I would not see her, for beholding thee,
 I am I know not what. If I have ought
 That may content thee, take it, and be gone,
 For death is not so terrible as thou,
 Thine eies shoote guilt into me.   85
ASPATIA.   Thus she swore
 Thou wouldst behave thy selfe, and give me words
 That would fetch teares into my eies, and so
 Thou doest indeed, but yet she bad me watch,
 Least I were cossend, and be sure to fight
 Ere I returnd.   90
AMINTOR.   That must not be with me,
 For her ile die directly, but against her
 Will never hazard it.
ASPATIA.   You must be urgd.
 I doe not deale uncivilly with those   95

That dare to fight, but such a one as you
Must be usd thus.

She strikes him.

AMINTOR.　I prethee youth take heed,
　Thy sister is a thing to me so much　　　　　　　100
　Above mine honour, that I can indure
　All this, good gods — a blow I can indure,
　But stay not, least thou draw a timelesse death
　Upon thy selfe.
ASPATIA.　Thou art some prating Fellow,　　　105
　One that has studied out a tricke to talke
　And move soft harted people; to be kickt,
　Thus to be kickt—

She kickes him.

　[*aside.*] Why should he be so slow
　In giving me my death?　　　　　　　　　　110
AMINTOR.　A man can beare
　No more and keepe his flesh, forgive me then,
　I would indure yet if I could, now show
　The spirit thou pretendest, and understand
　Thou hast no houre to live:　　　　　　　　115

They fight.

　What dost thou meane? thou canst not fight.
　The blowes thou makst at me are quite besides,
　And those I offer at thee, thou spreadst thine armes
　And takst upon thy brest, alas defencelesse.
ASPATIA.　I have got enough,　　　　　　　120
　And my desire, there is no place so fit
　For me to die as here.

Enter EVADNE. *Her hands bloudy with a knife.*

EVADNE.　*Amintor* I am loaden with events
　That flie to make thee happy, I have joyes
　That in a moment can call backe thy wrongs　　125
　And settle thee in thy free state againe,
　It is *Evadne* still that followes thee,
　But not her mischiefes.

AMINTOR.   Thou canst not foole me to beleeve agen,
   But thou hast lookes and things so full of newes   130
   That I am staid.
EVADNE.   Noble *Amintor* put off thy amaze,
   Let thine eies loose, and speake, am I not faire?
   Lookes not *Evadne* beautious with these rites now?
   Were those houres halfe so lovely in thine eyes,   135
   When our hands met before the holy man?
   I was too foule within, to looke faire then,
   Since I knew ill I was not free till now.
AMINTOR.   There is presage of some important thing
   About thee, which it seemes thy tongue hath lost: 140
   Thy hands are bloudy, and thou hast a knife.
EVADNE.   In this consists thy happinesse and mine;
   Joy to *Amintor*, for the *King* is dead.
AMINTOR.   Those have most power to hurt us that we love,
   We lay our sleeping lives within their armes.   145
   Why? thou hast raisd up mischiefe to his height,
   And found one, to out-name thy other faults;
   Thou hast no intermission of thy sinnes,
   But all thy life is a continued ill,
   Blacke is thy coulor now, disease thy nature.   150
   Joy to *Amintor*? thou hast toucht a life,
   The very name of which had power to chaine
   Up all my rage, and calme my wildest wrongs.
EVADNE.   Tis done, and since I could not finde a way
   To meete thy love so cleare, as through his life,   155
   I cannot now repent it.
AMINTOR.   Cudst thou procure the gods to speake to me,
   To bid me love this woman, and forgive,
   I thinke I should fall out with them: behold
   Here lies a youth whose wounds bleed in my breast,   160
   Sent by his violent Fate to fetch his death
   From my slow hand: and to augment my woe
   You now are present, stain'd with a Kings bloud
   Violently shed: this keepes night here,
   And throwes an unknowne Wildernesse about me.   165
ASPATIA.   Oh oh oh.
AMINTOR.   No more, persue me not.

EVADNE.   Forgive me then and take me to thy bed.

⟨*kneels.*⟩

We may not part.

AMINTOR.   Forbeare, be wise, and let my rage go this way.   170

EVADNE.   Tis you that I would stay, not it.

AMINTOR.   Take heed, it will returne with me.

EVADNE.   If it must be I shall not feare to meete it,

Take me home.

AMINTOR.   Thou Monster of crueltie, forbeare.   175

EVADNE.   For heavens sake looke more calme,

Thine eies are sharper then thou canst make thy sword.

AMINTOR.   Away, away, thy knees are more to me then violence,

I am worse then sicke to see knees follow me,

For that I must not grant, for Gods sake stand.   180

EVADNE.   Receive me then.

AMINTOR.   In midst of all my anger, and my griefe,

Thou doest awake something that troubles me,

And saies I lov'd thee once, I dare not stay,

There is no end of womans reasoning.   185

leaves her.

EVADNE.   *Amintor* thou shalt love me now againe,

Go I am calme, farwell; and peace for ever.

Evadne whom thou hatst will die for thee.

Kills herselfe.

AMINTOR.   [*Returnes.*] I have a little humane nature yet

Thats left for thee, that bids me stay thy hand.   190

EVADNE.   Thy hand was welcome, but it came too late,

Oh I am lost, the heavie sleepe makes hast.

She dies.

ASPATIA.   Oh oh oh.

v. III. 182 AMINTOR. In midst] *Amint.* I dare not stay, thy language,/In midst Q1–2. *The construction of this passage in* Qq *is ungrammatical, and the repetition of the first phrase three lines later suggests a false start uncorrected in the fair copy or a cancellation missed by both* Q1 *compositor and* Q2 *annotator. The speech makes perfect sense without the line.*

AMINTOR.   This earth of mine doth tremble, and I feele
   A starke affrighted motion in my bloud,   195
   My soule growes weary of her house, and I
   All over am a trouble to my selfe,
   There is some hidden power in these dead things
   That calls my flesh unto 'em, I am cold,
   Be resolute, and beare 'em company.   200
   Theres something yet which I am loath to leave,
   Theres man enough in me to meete the feares
   That death can bring, and yet would it were done,
   I can finde nothing in the whole discourse
   Of death I durst not meete the bouldest way,   205
   Yet still betwixt the reason and the act
   The wrong I to *Aspatia* did, stands up,
   I have not such another fault to answer.
   Though she may justly arme her selfe with scorne
   And hate of me, my soule will part lesse troubled,   210
   When I have paid to her in teares my sorrow,
   I will not leave this act unsatisfied,
   If all thats left in me can answer it.
ASPATIA.   Was it a dreame? There stands *Amintor* still,
   Or I dreame still.   215
AMINTOR.   How doest thou? speake, receive my love and helpe:
   Thy bloud climbes up to his old place againe,
   Theres hope of thy recoverie.
ASPATIA.   Did you not name *Aspatia*?
AMINTOR.   I did.   220
ASPATIA.   And talkt of teares and sorrow unto her.
AMINTOR.   Tis true, and till these happie signes in thee
   Staid my course, it was thither I was going.
ASPATIA.   Thou art there already, and these wounds are hers:
   Those threats I brought with me, sought not revenge,   225
   But came to fetch this blessing from thy hand.
   I am *Aspatia* yet.
AMINTOR.   Dare my soule ever looke abroad agen?
ASPATIA.   I shall sure live *Amintor*, I am well,
   A kinde of healthfull joy wanders within me.   230
AMINTOR.   The world wants lives to excuse thy losse,
228 lives] THEOBALD; lines Q1–2.

Come let me beare thee to some place of helpe.

ASPATIA.   *Amintor* thou must stay, I must rest here,
My strength begins to disobey my will.
How dost thou my best soule? I would faine live,   235
Now if I could, wouldst thou have loved me then?

AMINTOR.   Alas, all that I ams not worth a haire
From thee.

ASPATIA.   Give me thine hand, mine eyes grope and up downe,
And cannot finde thee, I am wondrous sicke.   240
Have I thy hand, *Amintor*?

AMINTOR.   Thou greatest blessing of the world, thou hast.

ASPATIA.   I doe beleeve thee better then my sense,
Oh I must goe, farewell.

AMINTOR.   She sounds: *Aspatia*. Helpe, for Gods sake water,   245
Such as may chaine life ever to this frame.
Aspatia, speake: what no helpe? yet I foole,
Ile chafe her temples, yet there nothing stirs.
Some hidden power tell her *Amintor* cals,
And let her answer me: *Aspatia* speake.   250
I have heard, if there be any life, but bow
The body thus, and it will shew it selfe.
Oh she is gone, I will not leave her yet.
Since out of justice we must challenge nothing,
Ile call it mercy if youle pittie me,   255
You heavenly powers, and lend forth some few yeeres
The blessed soule to this faire seat againe.
No comfort comes, the gods denie me too.
Ile bow the body once againe: *Aspatia*.
The soule is fled for ever, and I wrong   260
My selfe, so long to loose her companie.
Must I talke now? Heres to be with thee love.

Kils himselfe.

Enter SERVANT.

SERVANT.   This is a great grace to my Lord, to have the new

---

239 eyes grope] eyes grow Q1; hands grope Q2. *The Q2 annotator picked up* Q1
grow; *the Q2 compositor repeated* hand *from the same line. If her eyes were not in
question, Aspatia would not need to ask Amintor* (line 241) *if it is his hand she holds.*

King come to him, I must tell him he is entring. Oh God, helpe,
helpe.   265

Enter LISIPPUS, MELANTIUS, CALIANAX, CLEON,
    DIPHILUS, STRATO.

LISIPPUS.   Wheres *Amintor?*

STRATO.   O there, there.

LISIPPUS.   How strange is this?

CALIANAX.   What should we doe here?

MELANTIUS.   These deaths are such acquainted things with me,   270
    That yet my heart dissolves not. May I stand
    Stiffe here for ever: eyes call up your teares,
    This is *Amintor*: heart he was my friend,
    Melt, now it flowes, *Amintor* give a word
    To call me to thee.

AMINTOR.   Oh.   275

MELANTIUS.   *Melantius* cals his friend *Amintor*, oh thy armes
    Are kinder to me then thy tongue,
    Speake, speake.

AMINTOR.   What?   280

MELANTIUS.   That little word was worth all the sounds
    That ever I shall heare againe.

DIPHILUS.   Oh brother here lies your sister slaine,
    You loose your selfe in sorrow there.

MELANTIUS.   Why *Diphilus* it is   285
    A thing to laugh at in respect of this;
    Here was my Sister, Father, Brother, Sonne,
    All that I had, speake once againe,
    What youth lies slaine there by thee?

AMINTOR.   Tis *Aspatia*,   290
    My last is said, let me give up my soule
    Into thy bosome.

CALIANAX.   Whats that? whats that *Aspatia?*

MELANTIUS.   I never did repent the greatnesse of my heart till
        now,
    It will not burst at need.   295

CALIANAX.   My daughter, dead here too, and you have all fine
    new trickes to greive, but I nere knew any but direct crying.

MELANTIUS.   I am a Pratler, but no more.

⟨*Offers to kill himself.*⟩

DIPHILUS.   Hold Brother.

LISIPPUS.   Stop him.   300

DIPHILUS.   Fie how unmanly was this offer in you,
Does this become our straine?

CALIANAX.   I know not what the matter is, but I am growne
very kinde, and am friends with you all now. You have given me
that among you will kill me quickly, but ile go home and live as 305
long as I can.

Exit.

MELANTIUS.   His spirit is but poore, that can be kept
From death for want of weapons.
Is not my hands a weapon sharpe enough
To stop my breath; or if you tie downe those,   310
I vow *Amintor* I will never eate,
Or drinke, or sleepe, or have to doe with that
That may preserve life, this I sweare to keepe.

LISIPPUS.   Looke to him tho, and beare those bodies in,
May this a faire example be to me,   315
To rule with temper, for on lustfull Kings
Unlookt for suddaine deaths from God are sent,
But curst is he that is their instrument.

⟨*Exeunt.*⟩

FINIS

TEXTUAL NOTES

SIGLA

Q1 = Quarto, 1619; Q1^u = Q1 (uncorrected); Q1^c = Q1 (corrected).
Q2 = Quarto, 1622; Q2^u = Q2 (uncorrected); Q2^c = Q2 (corrected).
Q3 = Quarto, 1630.
Q4 = Quarto, 1638.
Q5 = Quarto, 1641.

THEOBALD = *The Works of Mr. F. Beaumont and Mr. J. Fletcher,
With notes by Mr. Theobald, Mr. Seward, and Mr. Sympson,*
vol. I. London 1750.

MASON = *Comments on the Plays of Beaumont and Fletcher, by
the Rt. Hon. John M. Mason.* London 1798.

DYCE = *The Works of Beaumont and Fletcher,* vol. I, ed. Rev.
Alexander Dyce. London 1843.

DANIEL = *The Works of Francis Beaumont and John Fletcher,*
vol. I, edd. A. H. Bullen, P. A. Daniel, etc. London 1904.

The caret mark ∧ is used throughout the Notes to indicate the absence
of punctuation; the wavy dash ∼ denotes the exact repetition of a
word given in the lemma.

I. I

3 are the brother] Q2; are brother Q1.

5-6 think'st thou of] Q1; think'st of Q2.

9 commend their King,] Q2; commend, Q1.

10 groome] Q1; Bridegroome Q2.

11 they'r] Q2; there Q1.

13-24 *Lined as prose in Qq. They comprise the last ten lines on the page in both substantive texts.*

15 blood abroad . . . peace.] Q2; blowes abroad bringst vs our peace at home, Q1.

18 be too kinde] Q2; be kinde Q1.

19 welcomes:] Q2; welcome, Q1.

20 worlds.] Q2; world. Q1.

37 Tis most true] Q1; Tis true Q2.

38 solemnities] Q1; solemnitie Q2.

41 I] Q2; and Q1.

41 those, that here] Q1; those∧ that Q2.

48 daunce with Armes:] Q2; daunce, Q1.

52 young my friend;] Q2; young; Q1.

53 is and temperate] Q2; is, Q1.

56-7 boast / I brought home conquest) he] boast) / I brought home conquest, he Qq.

62 Weigh it,] Q2; Weighes it, Q1.

64 *passing by.*] Q2; *passing with attendance.* Q1.

65 Q2 *adds a second speech heading for Melantius.*

75 mistaken, for] Q2; mistaken sir, Q1.

84 has] Q1; hath Q2

86 above] Q1; about Q2.

98 'a] Q1; he Q2.

99–100 If I could . . . / So] Q2; Could I but . . . / Such Q1. *Probably authorial tinkering.*

101–4 daughter. . . . / Discontented,] Q2ᶜ. stil his greatnes? / with . . . Q2ᵘ; daughter. / L I S. O t'were pittie, for this Lady sir, / Sits discontented Q1. *Q2's emendation seems to be an afterthought, since Q1 makes perfect sense, and the Q2 query about Calianax intrudes on the account of Aspatia. A foreshadowing of later developments in the story, it seems a clumsy piece of tailoring, but is unlikely to be other than authorial.*

105 The] Q2; In Q1.

106 And] Q2; Where Q1.

107 Shee with a sigh will tell] Q2; Then she will sit, and sigh, and tell Q1.

110 her over] Q2; them ouer her Q1.

114 sigh] Q2; swound Q1.

115 our] Q2; your Q1.

116 fill] Q2; fils Q1.

143 could no] Q2; could do no Q1.

150 those] Q2; these Q1. *Amintor's tears answer those of Melantius.*

151 wedding] Q1ᶜ; weding Q1ᵘ.

152 fickle] Q2; cruell Q1.

160–1 S.D. *Enter* MESSENGER. / MESSENGER.] Q2; AMINT. Q1. *This is probably a revision in fair copy. It was however left incomplete by the omission of the Messenger from the massed exit at line 163.*

163 S.D. *Exeunt . . .* DIPHILUS,] *Exeunt Lysippus, Cleon, Strato, Diphilus.* Q1; Q2 *omits the line completely, probably through eye-skip induced by Lisippus' listing of the names in the preceding line.*

163 STRATO.] *Strato* Q1ᶜ; *Steat* Q1ᵘ.

167 peace] Q2; sports Q1.

173 *Exeunt*] Q1; *Exit* Q2.

I. II

1 with] Q2; and Q1.

2 raile at] Q2; be angry with Q1.

3 i'th Court] Q3; i'th the Court Q1–2.

10–11 Pray stay, your] Q2; Your Q1.

12 asse you,] Q2; asse, Q1.

13 judgd] Q3; iudge Q1–2.

17 through my] Q2; through in my Q1. *Possibly a deliberate alteration by the* Q1 *compositor, who read* office *only as* position, *missing the wordplay and so normalising.*

18 And] Q2; But Q1.

21 there, there, so, so,] Q2; whose there, Q1.

21–3 *Knock within . . . Open*] What now? *within Knock within* / MEL. Open Q1–2. *Here as in lines 42 and 46 below, the stage direction* within *is located only approximately in* Q1 *and not corrected in* Q2.

24 Who's there?] Q2; Who i'st. Q1.

26 troope with you] Q2; troope Q1.

30 and theres] Q2; there is no Q1.

34 S.D. *Exit* MELANTIUS ⟨and⟩ LADY *other dore.*] Q1; om. Q2. *Two doors are necessary in this scene, and have caused the* Q2 *annotator to botch his correction. Melantius must leave by one door with his Lady at this point, and return (heralded by a speech from "within") 12 lines later. Calianax enters just before him, but, judging from his command to Diagoras to*

refuse entry to Melantius, not by the same door. Q1 gives a sufficient picture of the staging, Melantius and his Lady leaving by one door, Calianax entering by the other as Melantius calls from within, and Melantius then re-entering through the door by which he left. Q2 deletes both Melantius' exit (with that of his Lady) and his re-entry, leaving him on stage for Calianax's entry at the same time, incongruously, since he is still in Q2 supposed to call from within.

37 I,] Q2; no; Q1.

37–8 them for you:] Q2; them, Q1.

39 going away] Q2; giuing way Q1.

40 amongst them,] Q1–Q2^c; amongst, them Q2^u.

40–1 a dozen . . . his own] Q2; a dozen heads Q1.

46 MELANTIUS . . . CALIANAX] MEL. *Melantius? within Enter Calianax.* Q1; *Mel. Melantius. within Enter Calianax to Melantius.* Q2.

48 S.D. *Enter* MELANTIUS] *Enter Melantius* Q1; om. Q2.

50 you:] Q2^c; ∼, Q1–Q2^u.

58 vengeance, but be] Q2; vengeance, be Q1.

59–60 there so neere . . . King?] Q2; there. Q1.

66 thus] Q2; so Q1.

69 Why tis] Q2; Tis Q1.

70 shall forget] Q2; shall quite forget Q1.

71 live$_\wedge$ away] Q1^c; liue, away Q1^u.

74 Bate me] Q1; Bate Q2.

74 hee] Q2; of Q1.

83 that] Q2; the Q1.

86 or] Q2; and Q1.

89 say] Q2; talke Q1.

90 injurie] Q2; wrong Q1.

92 hand?] Q2; hands, Q1.

93 MELANTIUS] Q2; CAL Q1.

100 comming in] Q1^c; come in Q1^u.

105 KING. *Melantius*] King. Melantius Q2; Melantius Q1.

118 day can be unto me.] Q2; day, Q1. *Q1 ends with a comma not a full period, which suggests that the compositor may have been a victim of eyeskip. The abruptness of the speech, however, may rather imply an unclear cancellation in the copy for Q1.*

118 Maske] Q1; The Maske Q2.

119 come] Q2; now Q1.

119 raging] Q2; quenching Q1.

127 and how] Q2; that haue Q1. *A Q1 misreading of how as haue may have demanded the second change in an effort to make sense of the copy.*

129 I? I could not] Q2; I, can I not Q1. *The similarity of this and the following variant, together with the large number of verbal alterations, suggests authorial tinkering in this section.*

130 I am] Q2; am I Q1.

139 these mortals] Q2; those Q1.

143 hold] Q1; keepe Q2.

148–57 Yet whil'st . . . unquiet eyes.] Q2; om. Q1. *Probably a late insertion.*

152 wish] Q3; with Q2.

158 faire] Q2; pale Q1.

158 thy] Q2; that Q1.

159 crowne] Q2; fill Q1.

160 let] Q2; and let Q1.

162 then call] thine owne Q1; then call thine owne Q2. *A botched correction, the Q2 compositor printing both cancellation and correction.*

163 bed] Q2; banck Q1.

164 top . . . drawe away] brow . . . drawne away Q1; top . . . drawne away Q2. *It is possible that the manuscript read draw'm, which would be more grammatical, and would involve only a slight*

minim misreading by the Q1
compositor.

165   this . . . thy] his . . . thy Q1;
      this . . . this Q2. *The Q2 correction
      of Q1 his to this contaminated the
      later word.*

166   Queene] Q2; power Q1.

167   wine] Q2; winde Q1.

169   Turne] Q2; Turnes Q1.

171   nobler] Q1; noble Q2.

177   fetcht] Q2; force Q1.

185   his] Q1; thy Q2. *Either reading is
      possible, since Aeolus was some-
      times known as the son of the seas'
      King, and therefore with his
      winds was subject to him. But Q2's
      is the less familiar interpretation,
      and line 192's reference to* thy
      watrie race *(both* Qq) *shows
      Cynthia counterdistinguishing
      Neptune from Aeolus.*

191   welcomes] Q2; welcome Q1.

192–3 These are . . . Bring on] Q2;
      Bid them draw neere to haue thy
      watrie race / Led on Q1.

195   vessell] Q2; vessels Q1.

198   Oh,] Q2; See$_\Lambda$ Q1.

203   *Favonius*] Q3; *Fanonius* Q1–2.

205   Hee's too] Q2; Hee's Q1.

215–6 He will not . . . Maine] Q2;
      I will not be long thence, goe
      hence againe / And bid the other
      call out of the Maine Q1.

219   tell] DYCE; till Q1–2.

233   *rites*] Q2; *rights* Q1. *Cf.* II. I. 156.

244   *darke*] Q2; *old* Q1.

247   *blushes*] Q2; *losses* Q1.

252   *shrill*] Q2; *loud* Q1.

255   *though*] Q2; *if* Q1.

256–71 NEPTUNE. Great . . . are a
      twining] Q2; Maskers daunce,
      Neptune leads it Q1.

258   If not her measure] Q2. *Fleay
      (Chron. Eng. Drama,* I, 193)
      *ingeniously conjectured that the
      half-line is a misreading of a
      stage direction* Another measure.

*This would however be redundant
in view of the* measure *of line 263.
The speech can be glossed "I bring
this music to make this hour full
of pleasure if not fully an hour in
minutes".*

260   The . . . *Amphitrite*] Thy . . .
      Amphitrites Q2.

280   A thanks . . . gratulate] Q2; We
      thanke you for this houre, / My
      fauour to you all to gratulate Q1.
      *Neither text is satisfactory over
      these two lines, since they do not
      rhyme. Q1's mention of* this houre
      is pertinent, and rhymes with
      powre *in line 278.* Q1 *was
      basically correct but clearly under-
      went cursory revision, presumably
      authorial.*

283   and no] Q1; no Q2.

284   dwelling] Q1; dwellings Q2.

285   governments] Q1; gouernment
      Q2. *See preceding note; Cynthia is
      addressing all the maskers.*

286   charge] Q2; waters Q1.

288   NEPTUNE . . . *Gods*] Neptune . . .
      Gods. Q2; *Exeunt Maskers /
      Descend.* Q1. *The second part of
      the* Q1 *direction applies to Nep-
      tune, not the other Maskers.*

294   kingdomes] kingdome Q1; King-
      domes Q2.

298   must] Q2; dare Q1.

299   Heave up] Q2; Once heaue Q1.

301   set] Theobald; sect Q1–2. *Prob-
      ably foul case in* Q1, *since the* ct
      is a ligature.

301   whip] Q2; lash Q1.

302   same flashing] Q2; sun flaring Q1.

305   I into day. Adew.] Adew. Q1; I
      into day. Q2. *Q1's word was
      probably intended as the rhyme
      word to match* goe *in line 304,
      and was omitted as a consequence
      of a clumsy correction in Q2.*

305   *Finis Maske.*] Q2; *om.* Q1.

306   lights there Q2; light their Q1.

II. I

1–44 *There is probably corruption in the broken rhythms of this rhyming stichomythia, even if we take Evadne's replies as a set of prosaic refusals to play Dula's game.*

3 are very merry] Q2; are merry Q1.

6–7 EVADNE. Howes that?/...you doe.] Q1; *om.* Q2. *The absence of these lines interrupts what metrical flow there is.*

17 aright] Q2; right Q1.

18 Lady] Q2; Madame Q1.

19–20 FIRST LADY . . . Anon] I. LAD . . . Anon Q1; Q2 *gives both lines to Dula.*

21 You're] Q2; Tis Q1.

25 Tis high time] Q2; Tis time Q1.

31 I hope will take it] Q2; will take it I hope Q1.

42 Why doe I prethee.] Doe I prethee. Q1; Why doe. Q2. *A botched correction, the* Why *of Q2 being an authorial revision.*

45 couldst] Q2; coulst Q1.

71 See] Q2; Loe Q1.

73 into] Q2; vnto Q1.

75 and I feare 'm] Q1; I feare 'm Q2.

76 maist] Q2; must Q1.

79–97 ASPATIA. Lay . . . see you laid] Q2; *om.* Q1. *Authorial revision added to the fair copy.*

86 gentle] gently Q2.

100 no] Q2; not Q1.

121 You'le] Q2; Heele Q1.

122 bed yet,] Q2; bed, Q1.

137 OMNES.] *Om.* Q2; I. LAD. Q1.

140 Her] Q2; A Q1.

141 runne] Q2; raine Q1.

143 doe] Q2; did Q1.

148 that forst] Q2; inforst Q1.

150 is she] Q1; she is Q2.

154 will] Q2; shall Q1.

185 likes] Q2; will like Q1.

194 I sweare] Q2; sweete loue Q1. *Probably an authorial revision. It accords better with the phrase following.*

195 thee] Q2; it Q1.

197 with] Q2; to Q1.

199–200 This world . . . life to come] Q2; The world can yeeld Q1.

203–4 sin / Off from] Q2; sun / Of Q1.

205 I do know] Q2; I know Q1.

211 it then] Q2; it Q1.

212–3 shalt . . . shall not] Q2; should'st . . . cannot Q1. *This and other parts of the scene seem to have been subject to authorial tinkering.*

222 Thy] Q2; Her Q1.

225 *Amintor*] Q2; of these, what Q1.

227–8 Is this the truth, . . . hereafter.] Is this the truth, wil you not lie with me to night. / EUAD. You talke as if you thought I would hereafter. Q1; Will you not lie with me to night? / *Euad.* To night? you talke as if I would hereafter. Q2. *The correction of Q1 by the insertion of Evadne's* To night? *probably misled the Q2 compositor into thinking the phrase immediately above,* Is this the truth, *was cancelled. Amintor's reply* I doe *in the line following necessitates the second Q1 phrase* you thought, *which was omitted in Q2 through memorial failure or in an attempt to adjust the metre.*

233 thy] Q2; your Q1.

236 will] Q2; would Q1.

240 coynesse] Q2; kisses Q1.

248 that] Q2; whom Q1.

249 know, there's . . . that] Q2; know this, . . . then Q1.

256 can but] Q2; cannot Q1.

257 which] Q1; that Q2.

259 hand] Q2; paine Q1.
274 Instruct me in it] Q2; Instant me
       with it Q1.
279 her] Q2; their Q1.
284 those] Q2; that Q1.
284 armes—] ~. Q1–2.
322 act in practise,] Q2; act, Q1.
331 Northren] Q2; Northen Q1.
340 Tis] Q2; It is Q1.
343 name] Q2; word Q1.
356 What a strange] Q2; What strange
       Q1.
357 EVADNE] *Euad.* Q2; *om.* Q1.
361 live] Q2; loue Q1.
364 heart] Q2; breast Q1.
368 would] Q2; could Q1.
383 knew] Q4; know Q1–3.
386 through 'em] Q2; through, e'ne
       Q1.
387 lost] Q2; left Q1.
396 we] Q2; I Q1.
399 loving] Q2; longing Q1.
402 AMINTOR] *Amint.* Q2; *om.* Q1.
404 *Exeunt.*] Theobald; *Exit.* Q1–2.

II. II

 1   not sad,] Q2; not, Q1.
 2   Good gods,] Q2; Good, good, Q1.
12   nere] Q2; ere Q1.
12   *Olimpias*] Q2; *Olimpas* Q1.
13   an easie] Q2; a metled Q1. *See*
       Note on the Text.
16   Nor I] Q1ᶜ; Nere Q1ᵘ.
18–30 and bee sure ... oh that beast
       man] Q2; *om.* Q1. Q2, *doubtless*
       following the ms. insertion, prints
       as prose. The verse lineation given
       here is that followed by all editors.
22   but courts] TURNER; courts but
       Q1–2.
32   fine] Q2; faind Q1.
33   *Oenones*] *Oenes* Q1; *Ænones* Q2
35   fully] Q2; furie, Q1.
38   and having] Q2; hauing Q1.
49   backe] Q2; black Q1.
56   not] Q2; none Q1.
57   well exprest] Q2; exprest well Q1.

Both texts seem to be defective in
this passage.
58   so:] so, Q1–2.
59   *Antiphila,*] Q1; Q2 *locates this at*
       the end of the preceding line.
60   And over ... water,] Q1 *repeats*
       this line from the end of sig. E1 *at*
       the beginning of E1ᵛ, *possibly be-*
       cause the following line also begins
       And, *and so made the catchword*
       uncertain.
62   to the life] Q2; brauely Q1.
63   ANTIPHILA.] *Ant.* Q2; OLIM.
       Q1.
67   heere] Q2; there Q1.
67   *Antiphila*] Q2; *Antipila* Q1.
71   sad] Q2; poore Q1.
73   shall] Q2; will Q1.
74   And thinke ... breach now]
       Suppose I stand vpon the Sea,
       breach now Q1; I stand vpon
       the sea breach now, and thinke
       Q2.
76   that desart, and] Q2; the place
       she was in, Q1.
77   Tell that I am forsaken] Q2; Be
       teares of my story Q1.
79   strive ... looke] Q2; make me
       looke good girle Q1.
80   monument] Q2; mount Q1.
83   looke, looke] Q2; see, see Q1.
95   get ... worke,] Q2; in and
       whine there Q1.
97   doe that office] Q2; heat you
       shortly Q1.
98–9 My Lord ... thus in griefe,]
       Q2; Good my Lord be not
       angry, we doe nothing / But
       what my Ladies pleasure is, we
       are thus in griefe, Q1.
102 young] Q2; slie Q1.
105 way: what made an asse?] Q2;
       way, Q1.
106 will] Q2; must Q1. *The* Q2
       compositor inserted a further I will
       after whelps, *in line* 107, *probably*
       mistaking the ms. correction in Q1.

III. I

2　Oh] Q2; Our Q1.
6　None] Q1; No Q2.
20　have] Q2; did Q1.
22　We ventured] Q2; We haue ventured Q1.
26　aside.] Q1; om. Q2. *Both quartos are imperfect in their recording of asides.*
31–4　Your sister . . . another world] Qq *line as prose. Edd. lineate variously as verse.*
31　doth] Q1; does Q2.
32　their] Q2; the Q1.
33　chafe againe,] Q2; chafe, Q1.
37　does hee] Q1; he does Q2. *Either reading is possible, Q1 as an open retort, Q2 as an aside. The exclamation which begins Amintor's reply, however, gives the speech more obviously the character of a piece of play-acting in the speaker, so the transposition was probably in Q2, which gives the normalising order.*
38　not use to] Q2; not Q1. *Q2's correction adds a general profession of masculinity to the plain denial of Q1. The metre suggests that it is original.*
40　breath] Q2; breach Q1.
40　aside.] Q2; om. Q1.
56　the] Q2; this Q1.
59　ill. But] Q2; Ill. Q1. *Eyeskip in Q1 or possibly a deliberate omission, the compositor not recognising that the line was properly incomplete.*
60　Stay] Q2; Say Q1.
70–1　cals . . . shoots] Q2; call . . . shoot Q1.
74　But why,] Q2; Why, Q1.
95　I done? why] Q2; Why Q1. *Possibly an authorial insertion to emphasise Evadne's play-acting.*
102　aside.] Q2; om. Q1. *Eyeskip, or a late addition in the fair copy.*
114　lightned] Q2; heighned Q1.
123　how can I] Q2; can you Q1.
125　strange, *Amintor.*] Q2; strange. Q1.
126　s.d. *aside.*] *located after line 128 in Qq. Line 126 is run over to fill 127.*
127　too if] Q2; if Q1.
136　And] Q2; But Q1.
144　then, how . . . unto thee?] Q2; how then . . . to you. Q1.
168　aside.] om. Q2. Q1 *places the direction a line before, at the end of Amintor's speech.*
169　speech with you] Q2; speech Q1. *This speech, and the following one of Amintor, are only roughly lined as verse in Qq.*
172　Something heavenly . . . shall be] Q2; For it is Q1.
175　a jealous pang] Q2; iealous pangs Q1.
177　With whom] Q2; When Q1.
181　will and pleasure] Q2; pleasure Q1.
228　It] Q2; This Q1.
228–33　dissembling . . . *Amintor,*] Q2; dissembling, / *Amintor,* Q1. *This passage is clearly intrusive on the sense of Q1, and is presumably an authorial insertion.*
235　can'st] Q2; should'st Q1.
241　me] Q2; I Q1.
255　lied] Q2; lies Q1.
260–1　I send . . . / To show] Q2; I show Q1.
265　weight] Q2; waite Q1.
275　Waking] Q2; walking Q1.
280　hand] Q2; sword Q1.
283　were thousands fooles] Q2; are thousands Q1.
285　Iland] Q2; Land Q1.
290　it is my fate] Q2; is it my fault Q1.
294　beleevd] DANIEL; beleeue Q1–2.
306　Sounded] Q2; Seconded Q1.

308   Paines] Q2; Plagues Q1.

III. II

4   roome] Q2; part Q1. *On either reading, Melantius is expressing the wish that Calianax should die rather than Aspatia. Q1's word also allows the interpretation "supported her case," and was probably altered in the later copy because of this, since it makes Melantius express the wish that Calianax had supported his daughter against Melantius' sister.*

5   bloody treacherous slave.] Q2; bloody— Q1.

7   offices] Q2; office Q1.

10   Leave, some] Q2; Some Q1.

16–20   Why? . . . death can be.] *lined as prose in* Qq.

28   hath] Q2; hast Q1.

28   to] Q2; can Q1.

35–6   tricke, / I had mongst] Q1; tricke I had, / Amongst Q2.

40   aske] Q2; askt Q1.

42   will goe home and] Q2; will Q1.

48   Mens] Q2; Mans Q1.

48   not so] Q2; not Q1.

67   strove] Q2; striues Q1.

69   speech, or weare] Q2; speech— yow weare Q1.

71   cunning] Q2; tongue Q1.

80   Inevitable] Q2; Immutable Q1.

91   but] Q2; and Q1.

101   friend] Q2; friends Q1.

107   plaid] Q2; plead Q1.

111   injuries] Q2; miseries Q1.

117   that—] ∼, Q1; ∼. Q2.

149   tame?] Q2; tane, Q1.

151   strike] Q2; stick Q1.

169–70   borne, . . . happy.] Q2; knowne, . . . blessed. Q1.

175   scandall] Q2; farewell Q1.

188   wake] Q2; make Q1.

204   ease: Oh this] Q2; ease of this Q1.

223   thy] Q1; my Q2.

229   wrung] Q2; wrong Q1.

230   my] Q2; this Q1.

236   it from] Q1; it backe from Q2. *The extra word in Q2 is hyper-metrical, and was probably intro-duced by contamination from its reiteration two lines earlier.*

237–8   this, And . . . posterity:] Q2; this, Q1. Q2 *tacks the addition to the end of line 237.*

243   me be,] Q2; me, Q1.

264   buy] Q2; by Q1.

265   that] Q2; it Q1.

271   yet] Q2; but Q1.

274   our] Q2; your Q1.

278   me, and no more.] Q2; me. Q1.

305   hands to mine,] Q2; hands, Q1.

335–7   into your hatred . . . I come] Q2; into your idle hatred, / I am come Q1. *The Q2 compositor lines the addition after* hatred *as prose.*

354–5   or already . . . offered love] Q2; already, / The last is spoke, refuse my offerd loue Q1.

IV. I

1   God save you.] Q1; Saue you Q2. *God was frequently removed in the printing-house.*

6   commend] THEOBALD; command Q1–2.

9   into . . . tis] Q2; into a . . . it is Q1.

10   S.D. *Exit* LADY] *Exit Ladyes* Q1; *Exeunt Ladies* Q2. *The emenda-tion brings this* S.D. *into accordance with the entry of only one lady at the beginning of the scene.*

22   has it] Q2; has Q1.

56   they lied.] Q2; theile lie. Q1.

65   be sudden] Q2; come tell me Q1.

83   safer] Q2; *Safer* Q1.

85   foe] Q1; food Q2.

88–97   Force my swolne . . . a canker] *lined as prose in* Qq.

92–7   Thou hast . . . a canker] Q2; *om.* Q1. *An authorial addition.*

139 none else] Q2; no more Q1.

141 Oh . . . it was] Q2; *om.* Q1. *See following note.*

142 No more] Q2; *om.* Q1. *The conjunction of two major omissions so closely together in Q1 suggests that the ms. was marked in a way which indicated a cancellation to the Q1 compositor. Further such omissions occurring later in this scene however suggest either difficulties in reading the ms. at this point, or substantial authorial tinkering.*

148–9 EVADNE. Too long . . . sorry?] *Euad.* Too long . . . sorry? Q2; *Euad.* Too long, too late I finde it. / *Mel.* Can you be very sorry? Q1.

151 *Evadne,* thou wilt to] Q2; Woman thou wilt not to Q1.

155 Could'st thou not curse him] Could'st thee not curse him Q2; Has sunke thy faire soule Q1.

173 knew] Q2; had Q1.

180 great] Q2; thy Q1.

180 shalt] Q1; shall Q2.

185 full] Q2; foule Q1.

217 a new way . . . sorrowes,] Q1; no new way . . . sorrow Q2. *Compositorial interference is probable here as elsewhere in this scene; but which compositor it is difficult to say. Q1 makes more obvious sense, and its plural is clearly correct, as is shown by* many *in the line following.*

252 Can] Q2; Shall Q1.

272 win] Q2; get Q1.

288 am now] Q2; am Q1.

IV. II

19 Why if it be a lie] Q1; Why? if it be a lie Q2.

20 Ile be sworne] Q2; I besworne Q1.

39 in,] ~∧ Q1—2.

49 S.D. DIAGORAS] *Diag.* Q2; *om.* Q1. *The* Q1 *compositor was short of space here, and the* Q1 *stage direction fills its line, so he may have chosen to trim the text by deleting the last name in the line.*

56 chop] Q2; chopt Q1.

73 *aside.*] Q2; *om.* Q1.

101 besieg'd] Q2; beseidge Q1.

121 fault] Q2; faults Q1.

142–3 Pardon . . . preserve] Pardon me Sir, my bluntnesse will be pardoned, you preserue / Q1—2.

145 worth] Q2; world Q1.

159–60 didst thou not speake to me of it] Q2; that hast spoke to me / Of it Q1.

168 already] Q2; all ready Q1.

189–90 This sword . . . in peace;] Q2; *om.* Q1. *The shortness of the inserted second line may indicate an incomplete addition, either authorial or by an omission of the annotator.*

198 did not] Q2; did Q1.

203 *aside.*] Q2; *om.* Q1.

218 *Diagoras*] THEOBALD; *Mel. Diagoras* Q1—2. *This line is the first on the page in* Q1, *and repeats the speech-prefix of the last line on the previous page. The* Q2 *annotator failed to correct it.*

244 Tis] Q2; Too Q1.

250–2 And you . . . my friend,] *lined as prose in* Qq.

251 armes] Q2; arme Q1.

250–1 and beleeve / Thou] & beleeve / ~ Q2; thou Q1.

253 ever. Good] Q2; euer good Q1.

258–9 You cannot . . . about you.] Q2; You cannot . . . strongest / Part you haue about ye. Q1.

260 I doe] Q2; Dost not thou Q1. *The whole of this speech was probably overhauled in the fair copy.*

261 For I] Q2; I feele / My selfe Q1.

263 extremely] Q1; extraordinarily Q2.

264 melt] Q2; meet Q1.

265 Unkindnesses;] Q2; Vnkindnesse, Q1.

267 hurt!] Q2; wrong! Q1.

278 oth'King] Q5, oth'the King Q1–4.

291 *Melantius*, thou] Q1; Thou Q2.

303 for't] Q2; fort Q1.

362 for. Some plot] for some plot Q1; for. / Some plot Q2.

368 Why come] Q1; Why? come Q2.

v. I

3 and] Q2; and Sir Q1.

8–9 wake . . . thinkes—] ∼ . . . thinkes. Q1; Wake and then. Q2.

15 virgin] Q2; virtue Q1.

19 madnesse] Q1; daring Q2. *Probably a memorial failure in* Q2 *by contamination from* dare *two lines above.*

20 fooles,] Q2; mans Q1.

22 repent] Q1; preuent Q2.

25 oh God,] Q1; good heauens, Q2.

27 hath so long] Q2; has so farre Q1.

29 Tels me I merit in it] Q2; Confirmes me that I merit Q1.

31 rock] Q2; rake Q1.

32 seaze] Q1; take Q2. *Probably a memorial failure induced by the correction of* Q1 rake *immediately above.*

36 Ile strike] I strike Q1; Ile strick Q2.

40 I shall be strong enough.] Q2; As I beleeue I shall not, I shall fit him. Q1. *Evadne ends her soliloquy with a half-line before calling on the King to awake: probably a revision.*

50 What, doe . . . love?] Q1; What doe . . . loue, Q2.

53 see] Q2; looke Q1.

59 Here] Q1; There Q2.

68 How's this] Q2; How Q1.

117 villaine] Q2; villanie Q1.

129 S.D. *Exit*] *Exeunt* Q1–2. *The King and his bed must stay to be discovered by the Gentlemen. Probably an authorial slip.*

139 And so . . . well] Q2; *om.* Q1. *Probably an authorial elaboration.*

140 Treason, treason] Treason. Q1; Treason, Treason. Q2.

161 cals those] Q2; cals to those Q1.

v. II

19 certainly] Q2; certaine Q1.

33 pray to heaven] Q1; pray heauen Q2.

37–9 Some thinke . . . rascall.] Q2; I'm sure might haue preserued. Q1. *The* Q2 *compositor versifies Calianax's speech, which was added in revision.*

46 buy] Q2; begge Q1.

51 so) like my selfe,] Q2; so, like my selfe) Q1.

53 to revenge,] Q2; for reuenge, Q1.

79 you] Q2; the Q1. *Melantius is now addressing Lisippus. Probably the* Q1 *compositor misread a ms. abbreviation.*

v. III

5 die] Q2; doe Q1.

20 body.] Q2; but in particular, I haue in charge about no waightie matters. Q1. Q2 *makes adequate sense as it stands, and the passage is too considerable for its omission to be attributed to eyeskip: probably authorial revision.*
I] TURNER; he Q1–2.

52 not:] ∼, Q1–2.

54 hideous] Q2; odious Q1.

59 this houre I now arriv'd:] this houre, I now arriu'd, Q1–2. Q2's *customary adjustment of the punctuation becomes less thorough in the final section of the play.*

62 thing. She] ∼, she Q1–2.

64 her.] ∼, Q1–2.

67　though.] ∼, Q1–2.

69　againe;] ∼, Q1–2.

70　deale. The] ∼, the Q1–2.

72　publisht:] ∼, Q1–2.

82　what. If] ∼, if Q1–2.

95–8　You must . . . usd thus.] Q1
　　*lines as prose; Q2 accepts Q1's
　　lineation but capitalises the first
　　letter in each line.*

107　kickt,] ∼ₐ Q1–2.

115–9　Thou hast no houre . . . de-
　　fencelesse.] Q2; Q1 *lines* meane, /
　　. . . at me / . . . at thee / . . .
　　thine brest / . . . defencelesse.

123　*Her hands . . . knife.*] Q2; *om.* Q1.
　　*An authorial addition. See Com-
　　mentary note.*

130　lookes] Q1ᶜ; bookes Q1ᵘ.

131　staid] Q2; stald Q1.

134　beautious] Q2; beatious Q1.

150　nature.] ∼, Q1–2.

153　calme] Q2; tame Q1.

159　them:] ∼, Q1–2.

162–4　hand: and to . . . shed:] Q2;
　　hand, Q1.

168　*kneels.*] *om.* Q1–2. *It is evident
　　from lines 178–9 that Evadne is
　　kneeling to Amintor. She would
　　most aptly do so in begging for-
　　giveness.*

177　sharper] Q2; crueller Q1.

192　S.D. *She dies.*] Q2; *om.* Q1.

199　flesh unto] selfe vnto Q1; flesh
　　into Q2.

200　company.] ∼, Q1–2.

208　answer.] ∼, Q1–2.

265　CLEON] Q2; *om.* Q1.

294　of my heart] Q2; of heart Q1.

303–6　I know . . . I can] Qq *divide
　　this final speech of Calianax's into
　　rough verse, but his earlier
　　speeches are in prose, and it seems
　　better to make it so here.*

304　you all now.] Q1; you. Q2
　　*Probably the Q2 compositor trim-
　　med the line in an attempt to
　　improve the metrical pattern he saw
　　in the speech as a whole.*

306　S.D. *Exit.*] Q1; *om.* Q2.

COMMENTARY

I. I

2 STRATO] See Textual Note. The opening lines of the play are addressed by Cleon to the King's brother Lisippus; Strato, whose character throughout the play is that of a cynic, interjects, and Diphilus in the next lines reprimands him for his effrontery in interrupting the King's brother by asking Lisippus for his opinion ("weele take *your* word"). Lisippus, as the senior lord should, then soothes the contention by asking for Strato's views on the notion of a masque celebrating the wedding.

6 a maske] Masques were one customary and highly popular mode of celebration for a great event. They were frequently performed at Court, with professional actors complemented by Court lords and ladies. The scenery and costumes were lavishly expensive. Beaumont himself wrote a famous masque for his old Inn of Court, the Inner Temple, as its contribution to the celebrations for the marriage of the Princess Elizabeth to the Elector Palatine in 1613. Shakespeare's *The Tempest*, also containing a masque, was written at about the same time as *The Maid's Tragedy* for the same Company.

13 by me] Through me as its representative.

19 the time] The cause of his recall, the occasion of Amintor's wedding to Melantius' sister. Melantius at this point is unaware of his personal involvement with the wedding.

86 above her] i.e. is superior to Aspatia.

92 To honour you] This explanation of the strange alteration of the wedding plans provides the first use of the play's theme-word. The true motive for the King's action is totally dishonourable, and has the effect of dishonouring Melantius.

93 at his charge] Not only at his command but at his expense. Beaumont's Masque of the Inner Temple cost over £5,000, shared between Francis Bacon and the Benchers of the Temple.

137 build there] Build her nest there.

I. II

2-3 why very well said . . . i'th Court.] It is Calianax's office to stage-manage the presentation of the masque, which he does grudgingly, in view of his daughter's being slighted (lines 17–18) and of the effort involved. His notion is that if he performs his office badly the King will want the performance elsewhere.

118 *The Maske.*] Masques were always staged with considerable scenic elaboration, particularly for entries and exits. In this masque a trap is used for Night and Neptune to arise from, and for Neptune and the Sea Gods to leave by, and a rock covers one entrance, for Aeolus to emerge from. Cynthia and the dancers presumably enter normally. The mists in which Night appears were a common stage device. The choice of sea-gods and nocturnal figures is appropriate for a masque performed on an Aegean island, and for a play staged at an indoor theatre such as the Blackfriars, where night scenes were as easy to present as day scenes.

164   Latmus] A mountain in Caria (the South Turkish mainland North of Rhodes) where Endymion was discovered by Selene (Cynthia), who is said to have fallen in love with him and to have achieved for him the gift of immortality. In some versions he was granted eternal dreamless sleep. The reference to Endymion, underlined by the mention of Latmus, would have seemed appropriate in a play set in Rhodes.

243   Second Song] The irony implicit in the whole masque (not dramatic irony, since the audience cannot yet know the falsity of the picture represented) is most pointed in this song, where erotic convention draws on the assumption of the bride's virginity. The masque as a whole being the public celebration of the wedding serves both to stress the importance of the public event and to heighten the shock of the discovery of its hidden corruption. The public celebration is counterbalanced in the next act by Aspatia's private mourning.

295–7   I hope . . . drencht] Phaeton tried to drive the chariot of the sun, his father, on its diurnal course and, killed by a thunderbolt of Zeus when he allowed it too near the earth, fell into the river Eridanus.

II. I

7   That I might . . . doe] *i.e.* "That I

might go to bed with him with the licence which your marriage gives you." There is a suggestion of "reputation" as well as "warrant" in Dula's use of the term "credit".

35   Wilt take my place to night?] Part of an extended quibble on cardplaying, begun in line 29 when Evadne picks up Dula's word "trick" of lines 23 and 26. Dula takes Evadne's "place" to mean a place at a gaming table, not the marriage bed. To hold Evadne's cards means to play her hand in her absence. Offering to hold her cards "against any two I know" is an oblique compliment to Evadne's charms.

41   plucke downe a side] Cause the defeat of her own side.
She does not use it] A bawdy joke. She does not "use" her (sexual) "part".

50   But I could . . . Countrey] To pursue, follow up a scent, probably with a bawdy pun on the last word.

II. II

36   The *Carthage* Queene] Dido, founder of Carthage, who killed herself when abandoned by Aeneas.

42   Turnd her to Marble] like Niobe, who was turned into a weeping statue by the gods.

61   a feare] i.e. on the face of Theseus in this scene on the tapestry.

73   the wilde Iland] Naxos, where Ariadne was abandoned.

III. I

6–7   its ods against . . . while he lives] A double innuendo: the bridegroom of course "dies" in getting his bride's maidenhead; the secondary implication is that it is rare for a bridegroom to find a virgin bride. Strato has two cynical generalisations in the play, first in the opening scene, where he claims that masques are "tied to rules of flatterie", and secondly here. Each is eventually shown to be justified.

198–9 I love . . . my eies] This is the only speech of Evadne's to hint at her reasons for her liaison with the King. It is elsewhere accepted as lust.

252–4 Y'are a tirant . . . of it] This aspect of tyranny shows a markedly different face from the portrait of, for instance, the King in *Philaster*. The hypothetical problem, what to do when cuckolded by one's King, has far different requirements from the political problem, how to treat a tyrant who does not demand "things possible and honest", which is the more political, less personal question examined in *Philaster*.

260 your lives] The story of your lives. Many edd. accept Theobald's emendation "your lims".

III. II

248–53 it will be cald . . . cuckold] Amintor is making a difficult ethical point concerning revenge here: Melantius can shed his sister's blood honourably, in defence of his family name, and may have his revenge on the King in this way; but he must not shed the King's blood. Why Amintor should not with equal honour have killed his wife is not made clear. His awe of "the throne of Majestie" gives his character a suspicion of Hamlet-like evasion.

293 as sent] as if sent by Fate at this moment.

IV. I

14 millan skins] See *Valentinian*, II. II. 46–7: "guilded doublets / And Millan skins". Probably gloves made in Milan.

67 the dog] Sirius, the dog star, dominant in August, the month of heat and contagious sicknesses; "raines" means 'reigns', *i.e.* in the ascendant.

97 of a lovely rose, left thee a canker] This not uncommon image is later copied by Evadne in accusation against the King (v. II. 82–3).

113–14 tis a justice . . . base offenders] See *Othello*, v. II. 1–7. The echo of Othello's famous speech is a double one, since "tis a justice" is an almost exact parallel in meaning to "It is the cause".

164 To kill this base King?] The culmination of Melantius' dialectic. He has progressed from Evadne's sin to her shame, to her hatred against the cause of her shame and the impulse to curse the King, to the final message which has been the whole object of the scene in Melantius' mind. The persuasion of Evadne through the conflict of personal dishonour (the theft of her virtue) with public crime (killing the King) should be seen in terms of the dialectic between these two absolutes, dishonour and royal office. It is usual to see Evadne's reversal as the result of Melantius' skilful manipulation of the techniques of persuasion.

206 Would dare a woman] See *Hamlet*, IV. V. 133: "I dare Damnation . . . onely Ile be revenged".

236 any safetie] anything sure.

258 Lerna] The marsh in Argolis where the Hydra lived. "Nilus" in the same line anticipates the reference to crocodiles seventeen lines below.

268 Mocke not the powers above] Evadne expresses her penitence in explicitly Christian terms. Amintor's reproof is not simply a warning that she must repent sincerely but an implied reproof against her using the image of Amintor as her "Lord", Jesus-like casting light into her hell.

IV. II

44 The combat] Great quarrels could still, according to dramatic convention, be settled by means of a duel, as with the abortive combat of Mowbray and Bolingbroke in *Richard II*, I. III. The King's permission was required (see line 48).

324 Astronomers] Astrologers. Unless Melantius is hinting at cosmic warnings against his taking revenge there seems little point in this reference. It is not elaborated anywhere else in the play.

349–50 But tis the King . . . hees honest] A neat presentation of the moral question in its twin aspects: Amintor is too "honest" and therefore loyal to take his revenge; Melantius uses dishonest means to encompass his just ends. Melantius' dishonesty is stressed by his declared intention only 23 lines earlier to take his revenge on the King immediately, and by his outright lie in the final line of the scene. Amintor summarises the problem in lines 358–9.

V. I.

12 s.d. *King a bed*] The King's bed

is pushed out on to the stage, with the King asleep in it. See *Cymbeline*, II. II. I: "*Enter Imogen, in her Bed, and a Lady.*"

31 rock] To sleep, soothingly.

52 Ile be thy Mars] Mars, asleep with Venus (the "Queene of love") was trapped in a net by Vulcan, husband of Venus. The King acknowledges the adulterous aspect of the parallelism in suggesting they be caught together (line 53).

61 bleed] Evadne elaborates the conceit of herself as doctor, visiting the King to "know the state" of his body. A surfeited body was bled to purge it of its excesses. Hence the "physicke" she prescribed is, aptly, bleeding.

75 looke] a transitive usage common in Beaumont and Fletcher.

97 Those blessed fires] meteors.

103 weake catching women] Women were thought to be more liable to infection from the plague because of their inferior physique.

109 Within your cries] Within hearing of your cries, an ellipsis.

120 Oh.] More a groan of pain than an exclamation of surprise. Q1's stage direction for stabbing the King occurs here, probably on the assumption that a groan would accompany a stab-wound. It may be the mark of a second blow, since Evadne speaks of exchanging more of "these love-trickes". But this she must in any case do in killing him at line 127.

V. II

1 beleeve, I am arm'd.] Previous edd. have adopted the Q2 reading of this line, and thus have missed the appeal to the political power of the

masses familiar in most of the dramas of the collaboration. Here the "dull" people are less generously presented than in *Philaster*, written a year earlier, where it is the mob which places Philaster on his rightful throne. See lines 66–7 below.

46 buy] To purchase his support as an ally, and thus the military support of Melantius, his general.

58–68 The short . . . him the blanke] Melantius' honourable desire to be a subject is backed by a threat which belongs with *Realpolitik*; the urging of Lisippus by Strato similarly backs morality with expediency.

V. III

1 *in mans apparell*] and also, it would seem from the reference (line 45) to "these few blemishes", with her face scarred as if in battle.

48 would thou wert so too] That is, brother-in-law to Amintor by Amintor's marriage to Aspatia.

123 *Her hands . . . knife*] In view of the exchange between Amintor and Evadne which follows, there is an obvious irony in the stage business suggested by this late authorial addition: Evadne with her bloody knife entering to Amintor, who still presumably clutches his sword blooded on Aspatia.

BIBLIOGRAPHY

ABBREVIATIONS

D.A.	=	*Dissertation Abstracts*
E.M.	=	*English Miscellany*
P.B.S.A.	=	*Papers of the Bibliographical Society of America*
P.M.L.A.	=	*Publications of the Modern Language Association of America*
R.D.	=	*Renaissance Drama*
S.S.	=ʳ	*Shakespeare Survey*
S.B.	=	*Studies in Bibliography*

I. WORKS OF BEAUMONT AND FLETCHER

A. COLLECTED AND SELECTED EDITIONS

The Works of Beaumont and Fletcher, in 11 vols, ed. Rev. Alexander Dyce. London 1843–6.

The Works of Francis Beaumont and John Fletcher, in 4 vols. (incomplete), edd. A. H. Bullen, P. A. Daniel, R. Warwick, etc. London 1904–12.

The Works of Francis Beaumont and John Fletcher, in 10 vols., edd. Arnold Glover and A. R. Waller. London 1905–12.

"*The Maid's Tragedy*" and "*Philaster*", ed. A. H. Thorndike. Boston 1906.

B. THE MAID'S TRAGEDY

The Maides Tragedy. First Quarto 1619; Second Quarto 1622.

The Maid's Tragedy, ed. F. J. Cox. London 1908.

II. STUDIES OF BEAUMONT AND FLETCHER

A. GENERAL

1. *Textual*

BOWERS, FREDSON. *On Editing Shakespeare and the Elizabethan Dramatists.* Cambridge (Cambridge U.P.) 1955.

2. *Critical*

APPLETON, W. W. *Beaumont and Fletcher, A Critical Study*. London (Allen and Unwin) 1956.

BENTLEY, G. E. "Shakespeare and the Blackfriars Theatre", in *S.S.*, I (1948), p. 38–50.

DANBY, J. F. *Poets on Fortune's Hill*. London (Faber) 1952. Reissued as *Elizabethan and Jacobean Poets* in 1964.

FERMOR, UNA ELLIS. *The Jacobean Drama*. London (Methuen) 1936.

LEECH, CLIFFORD. *The John Fletcher Plays*. London (Chatto and Windus) 1962.

MAXWELL, BALDWIN. *Studies in Beaumont, Fletcher, and Massinger*. Chapel Hill (U. of N. Carolina Press) 1936.

MINCOFF, MARCO. "The Social Background of Beaumont and Fletcher", in *E.M.*, I (1950), pp. 1–30.

———. "Fletcher's Early Tragedies", in *R.D.*, VII (1964), pp. 70–94.

ORNSTEIN, ROBERT. *The Moral Vision of Jacobean Tragedy*. Madison and Milwaukee (U. of Wisconsin Press) 1965.

PETTET, E. C. *Shakespeare and the Romance Tradition*. London (Staples Press) 1949.

RULFS, DONALD J. "Beaumont and Fletcher on the London Stage, 1776–1833", in *P.M.L.A.*, LXIII (1948), pp. 1245–64.

SPRAGUE, A. C. *Beaumont and Fletcher on the Restoration Stage*. Cambridge, Mass. (Harvard U.P.) 1926.

THORNDIKE, ASHLEY H. *The Influence of Beaumont and Fletcher on; Shakespeare*. Worcester, Mass. (Oliver B. Wood) 1901.

WAITH, EUGENE M. *The Pattern of Tragicomedy in Beaumont and Fletcher*, in *Yale Studies in English*, No. 120. New Haven (Yale U.P.) 1952.

WALLIS, LAWRENCE B. *Fletcher, Beaumont and Company*. New York (Kings Crown Press) 1947.

B. *THE MAID'S TRAGEDY*

1. *Textual*

HOY, CYRUS. "The Shares of Fletcher and his Collaborators in the Beaumont and Fletcher Canon (III)", in *S.B.*, XI (1958), pp. 85–106. *The Maid's Tragedy* is discussed on p. 94.

NORLAND, H. B. "The Text of *The Maid's Tragedy*", in *P.B.S.A.*, LXI (1967). pp. 173–200.

STILLMAN, D. G. "A Critical Textual Study of Beaumont and Fletcher's *The Maid's Tragedy*". Unpublished dissertation (University of Michigan) 1942.

TURNER, ROBERT K. JR. "The Relationship of *The Maid's Tragedy* Q1 and Q2", in *P.B.S.A.*, LI (1957), pp. 322–7.

——. "A Textual Study of Beaumont and Fletcher's *The Maid's Tragedy*", in 2 vols. Unpublished dissertation (University of Virginia) 1958.

——. "The Printing of Beaumont and Fletcher's *The Maid's Tragedy* Q1 (1619)", in *S.B.*, XIII (1960), pp. 199–220.

2. *Critical*

BARBER, CHARLES L. *The Idea of Honour in the English Drama*, 1591–1700, in *Gothenburg Studies in English* VI, ed. Frank Behre. Göteborg (Almqvist & Wiksell) 1957.

LAIRD, DAVID. "The Inserted Masque in Elizabethan and Jacobean Drama", in *D.A.*, XV (1955), p. 2527.

GLOSSARY

Amphitrite	*sea goddess, wife of Neptune,* I. II. 260.
anon	*soon, now,* III. II. 313.
Ariadne	*lover of Theseus, abandoned by him on Naxos,* II. II. 44.
Aspicks	*asps, small poisonous reptiles,* II. II. 27.
Bate	*except for,* I. II. 74.
baud	*pandar, pimp,* III. I. 303.
breach	*beach,* II. II. 74.
blanke	*paper not written on,* V. II. 68.
blast	*split, blight,* IV. II. 258.
blaze	*proclaim, make known,* II. I. 378.
Boreas	*the North wind,* I. II. 186 etc.
brable	*quarrel over trifles,* I. II. 107.
brother	*brother-in-law,* III. I. 16.
catch	*song, a round,* III. I. 110.
change	*exchange,* V. I. 115.
chop out	*rush out with (a merry tale), gabble,* IV. II. 56.
Cinthia	*Diana, the moon,* I. II. 121 etc.
codes	*Gods,* I. II. 21.
counterfeit	*pretend, dissemble,* III. II. 291.
course	*(in or by) turn,* I. I. 116 etc.
cousening	*cheating, dissembling,* II. II. 46 etc.
coxcomely	*stupid, clownish,* I. II. 12.
dare	*defy, outstrip the capacity of,* IV. I. 206.
discover	*uncover, reveal,* I. II. 126 etc.
disperse	*spread,* V. I. 102.
doate	*be senile, live out one's dotage,* III. II. 16 etc.
Endimion	see Commentary note to I. II. 162
Eolus	*God of the winds,* I. II. 197 etc.
facing	*brazening it out,* IV. I. 66.
Favonius	*Zephyrus, the West wind,* I. II. 203.
fond	*foolish,* I. II. 78.
forsworne	(a) *proved a liar,* (b) *made to break an oath,* I. II. 7.
gamesome	*sportive, frolicsome,* I. I. 42.
gratulate	*render thanks,* I. II. 281.
hand-wolfe	*a tamed wolf,* IV. I. 221
hang	*be hanged, hang yourselves,* I. II. 58.

hazard	*take the risk of,* II. I. 314.
headsman	*executioner (of maidenheads),* III. I. 32.
Hesperus	*the evening star,* I. II. 270.
hoboies	*hautboys, wind instruments,* IV. II. I.
honest	*chaste,* III. I. 142 etc.; *honourable,* IV. II. 350 etc.
honour	*reputation,* II. I. 380 etc.; *chastity,* III. II. 138 etc.
humorous	*moody, irritable,* DR. PER. etc.
huswives	*worthless girls,* II. II. 91.
Hymen	*the god of marriages,* I. II. 264 etc.
ingenious	*ingenuous,* III. I. 233.
leaprous	*marked by leprosy,* IV. I. 223 etc.
Lethe	*the waters of forgetfulness, a river in Hades,* III. I. 27.
measure	*a dance,* I. I. 45 etc.
motes	*minute particles,* II. I. 330.
Niobe	see Commentary note to II. II. 42.
Oenone	*the nymph abandoned by Paris,* II. II. 33.
office	*the official position, the official robe,* I. II. 15.
palsey	*tremulous paralysis in the aged,* I. II. 68.
Phoebus	*the sun personified, Apollo as sun-god,* I. II. 155.
pickthanks	*a sycophant,* III. I. 244.
policie	*shrewdness, prudence,* III. II. 365.
practise	*maintain a deception,* II. I. 398.
prating	*chattering,* III. I. 311 etc.
Proteus	*a sea-god, master of changing shapes,* I. II. 217.
push	*(an exclamation) pish,* III. I. 97.
quick	*lively,* III. I. 150; *alive,* III. II. 203.
quicknesse	*sharpness,* I. I. 61.
raile	*abuse, express anger,* I. II. 2 etc.
resolute	*convinced,* III. I. 309.
restie	*rancid, tainted* (dial.), II. II. 96.
returne	*turn back* (trans.), I. II. 27.
scurvily	*contemptibly,* III. I. 130 etc.
solemnities	*ceremonies,* I. I. 38 etc.
sounds	*swoons,* V. III. 245.
stale	*a has-been,* II. II. 106; *worn out, no longer fresh,* IV. I. 169.
stamp	*impression, die-stamping,* II. II. 13.
stout	*brave, fierce,* III. II. 32.

successively	*in succession, lineage*, I. I. 70.
swenge	*beat, scourge*, II. II. 93.
temper	*temperament*, II. I. 222 etc.; *hardness of metal*, II. II. 13.
testie	*irritable, contentious*, I. II. 94 etc.
timelesse	*untimely*, I. II. 53 etc.
Tritons	*sea-gods, children of Neptune and Amphitrite*, I. II. 262 etc.
troth-plight	*betrothed*, DR. PER.
truls	*prostitutes, wenches*, I. II. 36.
uncollected	*uncontrolled, irrational*, IV. II. 357.
unexprest	*inexpressible*, III. II. 86.
vernall	*suggestive of Spring*, I. II. 189.
vilde	*vile*, I. II. 90 etc.
winke	*turn a blind eye*, III. I. 301.